MW01048356

Freeing the Corporate Mind

Freeing the Corporate Mind:

How to Spur Innovation in Business

by

Arthur W. Cornwell

Execu-Press / Rockford, Illinois

First printing 1992
Printed in the United States of America

Library of Congress Cataloging in Publication Data

Cornwell, Arthur W., 1941-
Freeing the corporate mind: how to spur innovation in business / by Arthur W. Cornwell.
p. cm.
Includes index.
ISBN 0-9630807-0-9 : $19.95
1. Creative ability in business. I. Title.
HD53.C67 1992
658.4–dc20 91-42441
CIP

About the Author

Art Cornwell has 28 years of professional experience. He has been the president of two firms, and the marketing vice-president of three others. Art has launched two businesses of his own, and is currently the president of The Boardroom, a training and consulting firm he started in 1976.

For the past five years, Art has conducted over 100 presentations per year in virtually every English-speaking country. He is a member of the National Speakers Association and Public Speakers of Illinois.

Convinced that American innovative ability was the best tool for resuscitating the economy, Art began specializing in showing business professionals how to think more innovatively in 1985. Since this book is based to a large extent on the contributions of business people attending his seminars, Art always welcomes contact from participants. Please feel free to contact Art at:

The Boardroom
321 W. State St., Suite 308
Rockford, IL 61101
815-962-7100

This book is available for customized design to reinforce company goals in innovation or employee involvement.

Acknowledgments

Writing a book is a surprisingly lonely task. There are times during the process that the book, initially a noble and worthy goal, becomes an albatross. Without the spirited encouragement of friends and business associates, I doubt that many of us would complete the job.

I have been fortunate to have a bevy of friends who developed the ability to sense when my commitment was weakening. To them I owe a debt of gratitude, as they were always there to spur me on.

Among these, several stand out as not only spiritual prompters, but also beneficial critics of my work. Jim Powers and Larry Smeltzer both were generous with their suggestions. This book has been improved through their comments.

My special gratitude goes to Jon Lundin, who offered constructive criticism at such a fluid rate it gave cause to question his regard for our relationship. Our relationship has actually been enhanced by his candor, as has this book.

Of course, my greatest thanks has to go to those thousands of business people who have attended my seminars on business innovation, for without their constant ideas and suggestions, the need for this book would have never become apparent to me.

Writers who have dealt with this subject in the past have also provided information and inspiration for *Freeing the Corporate Mind*. Dr. Arthur Van Gundy, Roger

VonOech, and Edward deBono were particularly helpful, as many of the ideas presented in their books form the basis for the techniques offered here. The creativity exercises offered in books by Eugene Raudsepp also helped to provide clarification of concepts in innovation.

In the process of developing our personal skills, we all develop a store of recalled information. While we may have that information for the rest of our lives, we rarely remember its origin. The information has become part of our general body of knowledge. Much of what I know about helping people become more innovative I have learned from others, and I would like to give proper credit for that. Unfortunately, I don't always remember the source of that information, and proper credit is impossible. To those I may have forgotten, I extend my apologies and thanks.

The graphics used to demonstrate ideas throughout this book were done by Chris Mann, and the original manuscript was entered by Kathy Newton.

Table of Contents

Why Innovation?

In the early 1970's the United States became enamored with a book from Richard Bach entitled *Johnathon Livingston Seagull*. In his book, Bach describes the difficulties experienced by his seagull character, Johnathon Livingston Seagull.

Always aiming for higher personal goals, Bach's hero finds that through practice and continually challenging accepted limits, he is able to dive like a hawk, soar like an eagle, and fly faster than any bird before him. All very unseagull-like skills.

As a consequence of his breakthroughs, Johnathon is rejected by his peers and questioned by his family. Despite this rejection, Johnathon finds the call of constant challenge, improvement and change too strong to ignore. He continues to resist conformity and predictability in exchange for reaching new heights of flying skill.

Only when permitted to a higher life is Johnathon surrounded by his peers; those who appreciate his accomplishments and encourage his continued growth.

Why were American readers so taken by this comparatively short story of a deviant seagull? Poor Johnathon wasn't even an endangered species!

American readers saw in Johnathon Livingston Seagull a piece of themselves, that small chunk of our heritage that ordains us always to grow and change, to challenge that which is accepted in favor of something better.

Americans subtly recognize that this country was built entirely on the risks of the innovator.

The people who originally settled this country took an enormous risk in simply making the trip. Their success here would be largely determined by their ability to mold the opportunity here. Later, as the country developed, innovative industrialists started what would become the world's foremost economic power, the United States economy.

The impact of this growth has been international. Today the industrial strength of any country is measured primarily by its productivity in two sectors: automotive and communication. Both of these industries began commercially in the United States, and were based on American innovation! Innovation is woven throughout our history.

Now our own innovations are being used by our international competitors to penetrate our consumer and industrial markets. Watching these markets erode, we now hear the call to emulate international competitors. This call to emulate ignores two significant facts.

First, if our lead internationally was created through innovation, why would we abandon that inherent strength to try to copy others? It is true that we have a great deal to learn from our international neighbors. We can learn style from the Italians, patience from the Chinese, discipline from the Germans, and interpersonal style from the Japanese. Learn from, yes; emulate, no! Our unique strength has always been innovation and creativity; we shouldn't abandon it now.

Secondly, it is impossible to try to copy a national strength without that national heritage. To duplicate the Japanese, we would have to be raised in a culture that offered the same characteristics as the Japanese culture. We clearly were not.

This country is better positioned than any other to encourage innovation from its citizens, but that strength has been put aside.

Today, futurists tell us that it is impossible to predict the future by extrapolating the past, things are happening too fast for that. How could anyone predict the phenomenal growth of personal computers? What seer could have foreseen the fall of the Berlin Wall when it happened?

More than at any time in our history, we are being pressed to verify our international leadership. Our response has been candidly disappointing so far. We are scrambling around trying to defend ourselves from the incursion of international products, rather than asserting our continued leadership through new innovations. To arrest this confusion, we need to learn to take advantage of our innate strength, that of commercial innovation.

We are also turning to our employees and asking them to provide innovative ways to improve what we have done in the past. Gain sharing, profit sharing, and all attempts at employee participation will succeed or fail largely on the basis of their ability to find new solutions.

That is the purpose of *Freeing the Corporate Mind.* In the pages that follow, we will look at the things that have caused us to be less creative over time, their impact on us, and what we can do about it. We'll also review tools to use for increasing our personal creativity. Most importantly, we'll develop our personal skills in innovation, and those of others around us.

In the Websters New World Dictionary, the term "innovate" is defined as "to introduce new methods, devices."

This same dictionary defines "creative" as "having or showing imagination and artistic or intellectual inventiveness."

In this book we will use these terms interchangeably, for reasons which will become obvious in later chapters.

In recognition of the number of women currently active in the successful operation of business, we use both he and she in this text to refer to the species, and not the sex of the subject. We hope this does not confuse the reader.

Chapter One: Setting the Stage

While most authors hope that their books will be picked up and read from cover to cover in one sitting, that is not the aim of this book. To fully understand and apply the information in this book, we suggest reading sections one at a time, applying that information, and then moving on when you are ready. To assist in doing this, each chapter will be preceded by a summary of the previous chapter and a list of objectives to which the next chapter will respond. By organizing the book in this fashion, you can quit reading at any time and later get back to the book at your leisure, without having to worry about forgetting key points. In addition, you can review the summaries and objectives of all previous chapters to be certain you have not missed key points.

Since this is the first chapter, we do not offer a summary, but our objectives for Chapter One are as follows:

1. Identify the impact our prior experience has on our ability to think innovatively.
2. Define an innovative idea.
3. Explain the stereotypes people have of creative individuals.
4. Show how the American perception of innovation differs from that of other countries.
5. Indicate where innovation fits in our current decision-making techniques.

6. Show what actually happens during our creative insights.
7. Review our barriers to thinking creatively.
8. Point out the drawbacks of education and experience in generating creative ideas.

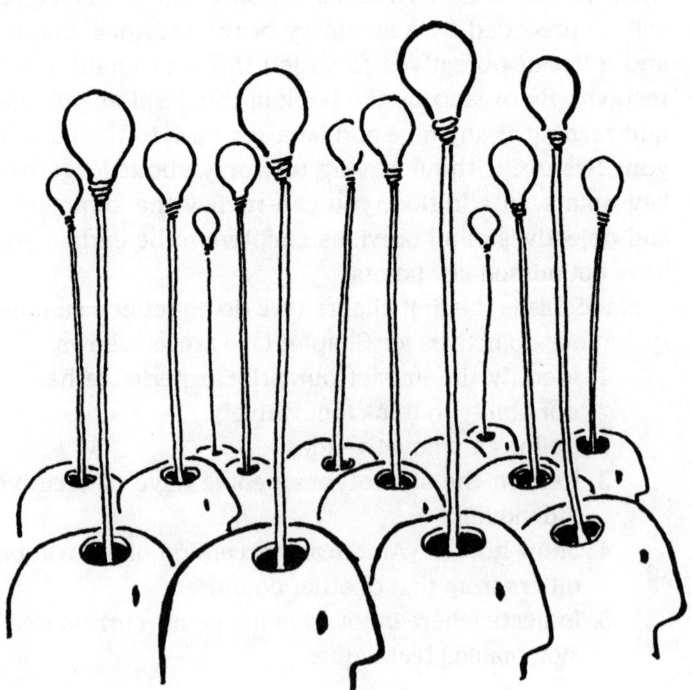

Can you imagine what our lives would be like today if our ancestors had been more creative? I'm not even suggesting that they should have been revolutionary in their thinking. What if they had been sufficiently creative to generate new ideas a mere ten years earlier?

We've been told that knowledge grows geometrically rather than arithmetically. If that is true, imagine what our current lives would be like if today's innovations had been generated only ten years earlier.

- Could we control the effects of gravity?
- Would we have access to friction free surfaces?
- How would superconductivity affect our daily lives?
- How many new millionaires would we have as a result of the above innovations?
- What new products would we have now?
- How would our lives be made easier?

Ten years seems like such a modest objective that we should have no trouble meeting it. For a number of reasons, all within our control, I suspect that reaching such a goal of advanced thinking will be very difficult. This type of innovative leap into the future requires a great deal of mental flexibility, and few of us have that attractive characteristic.

Not that any of us are incapable of creating innovative ideas. The fact is, we all are inherently capable of it. Over time, however, a number of events have taken place which have boiled the creative juices out of us. In the first section of this book, we'll discuss each of these events. As we discuss them, I suspect you will be able to see how they have affected your approach to creative thinking; how they have in fact caused you to be rigid in your approach to new ideas.

Certainly one problem in the development of our creative abilities is the lack of necessity. We are basically quite comfortable in thinking as we do; the need to be more creative isn't at all apparent. As a result of our maturation and our increasing ability to judge, we find that we are completely capable of solving problems. Over the years we have been able to survive and prosper in our jobs with the mental powers we currently have at our disposal. Similarly, we have been able to handle most domestic situations as they come up. No, our solutions to all problems aren't perfect, but they normally are good enough to get us by with some level of comfort.

This being the case, why should we bother to change the way we think? My suspicion is that you already have the answer to that or you wouldn't have picked up this book. If there is a better way of doing something, you'd like to find it. If there are new ideas to develop, you'd like to develop them.

What are some of the reasons that we don't think as creatively as we might?

The first, and one of the most significant, is the impact on our thinking of what I call "priors."

How "Priors" Limit Our Creativity

Things that have happened to us in the past form the framework for our future thinking. We believe that the future is an extension of the past. This inaccurate assumption limits our ability to innovate.

PRIORS

In 1927, Jack Warner of Warner Brothers Studios said, "Who in hell wants to hear actors talk?"

In 1899, in announcing his resignation as Director of the U.S. Bureau of Patents, Charles Duell said, "Everything that can be invented has been invented."

In 1905, Grover Cleveland, then President of the United States, said, "Reasonable and intelligent women don't want to vote."

What made these statements so shocking was not so much that they were foolish, which they were. What made the statements shocking was that they were uttered by individuals who knew what they were talking about. These weren't idle statements made by the poorly informed.

Jack Warner probably knew as much about the movie industry as anyone in the world when he offered the above observation. Similarly, who could have known more about the proliferation of patents than Charles Duell? Or known more about the needs of his constituents than the President of the United States?

All of these statements, along with many that we make, are the result of "priors." In the field of criminology, the term "priors" refers to a pattern of consistent performance by a criminal. By evaluating their priors, it is possible for law enforcement officers to anticipate future behavior of criminals, and accurately assign crimes to particular individuals.

In the context of creativity, the term priors refers to judgments we have made in the past, and our tendency to continue with those same judgments in the future. Our prior ideas become our present and future ideas. Jack Warner, Charles Duell, and Grover Cleveland all applied their previous logical thinking to an issue that required fresh thinking, and they all ended up saying something that history would treat unkindly.

Sometimes we don't appreciate how many of our current ideas are lodged in the past. Look for a moment at the development of population centers of the world. Initially, people lived in close proximity for protection. This was because they thought it would be easier to defend themselves from invaders if they were close to one another. As commerce became more significant, these concentrations of population tended to be on commercial waterways, either oceans or navigable rivers.

Today the population tends to remain concentrated, despite the fact that we know the drawbacks of compressing space around people. In addition, these population concentrations tend to remain on waterways, despite the fact that rail transport is significantly more important than water. These cities were all built on the basis of priors. Yet the cities remain, despite information which indicates that this concentration of people is no longer wise.

The development of the automobile also follows the pattern of prior concepts. In its initial development, the automobile became a four-wheeled vehicle powered by an internal combustion engine. These dimensions, as you know, apply to all automobiles. This is the case despite the attractiveness of three-wheeled vehicles powered by steam or electricity or . . .?

In looking at the impact of priors on your thinking, this may all seem a bit abstract. Let's see if you experience some of the same restricted thinking applied in your day-to-day logic. As a dutiful employee, you have likely learned that it is best to determine the position of your boss on a particular issue before stating your own position. Survival, after all, tends to grow from such an approach. What happens, then, when you become the boss, and the old predisposition of waiting before announcing is inappropriate? We have to make a conscious adjustment for the removal of that prior. Many of us find it impossible to make that adjustment after years of "prior" experience.

The same is no less true in raising our children. In the early stages of their development, we have no difficulty convincing them that it is we who establish rules—rules we expect them to follow. As they enter their middle and late teens, our children see rule-making as something in which they have a right to participate. Based upon our prior method of handling the development and enforcement of rules, this required change in approach presents a problem for many parents.

The point is simply this: to a much greater extent than we believe, prior notions about the way things should be done affect our current approach, and serve to restrict our mental flexibility.

The Restriction of Habits

When we are acting out of habit rather than deliberate choice, our brains are not involved in that activity. As a result, our habits also reduce our creative abilities.

Generally speaking, you and I develop habits to save us the burden of having to rethink everything. Frequently we are not aware of the impact habits have on a major share of our lives. For simple example, look at the way you begin your day. Habit is so pervasive I'll wager that when you get up in the morning you don't have to think about anything until you get to work. Everything in your morning has been reduced to habit. If necessary, you could go through your morning routine essentially "brain-dead," and you have likely done so on several occasions.

You drive to work the same way every day. If you were the second person in your family to take your shower this morning, you are the second person every morning; and the first day that you want to take the first or third shower, you will mess up the schedule of everyone in your family.

Even your morning sequence of dressing is dominated by habit. If a man puts on his right sock first this morning, he puts on his right sock first every morning. The first morning he tries to put on his left sock before his right, he's going to fall on his face!

Habits get to be absolutely overpowering. For example, ever since you were a child, your mother told you to look both ways before crossing the street. Tell me, what do you do as a result of this intensive training when you come to a one-way street? You look both ways, right?

That habit doesn't work for you on a one-way street, yet you obediently continue to use it. You never stop and say to yourself, "that habit didn't work this time, so I'll reevaluate the situation before I do something this stupid again." You continue to use the habits that you have developed. You become so dependent upon those habits that you stop reviewing them, never asking yourself if you should discontinue or change them.

This is not to attack all habits, or suggest that they should be dismantled. Not at all. Habits get us to work on time, help us coordinate with other members of the family, and generally make our lives easier.

However, when they dominate so much of our thinking that we become mentally numb, we lose our mental flexibility. At that point, we cease to consider optional ways of doing things.

To give you an example of how important habits become to us, think back to your first day on the job with your current employer. The first day was incredibly confusing. You didn't know where anything was, who to talk to for information, where to go for lunch (or the washroom, for that matter), where everyone belonged in the organization, and where the misfits were. Not only that, but at the end of that first day you were absolutely exhausted.

The reason you were so tired at the end of the first day

was because everything you did during the course of that day forced you to select one from many options. Even an issue as simple as when to schedule an appointment with your boss was an unknown. In other words, you were exhausted from excessive mental activity. You had no habits or routines to help you through the day.

The second day was somewhat easier because you could remember some of the right choices you had made the day before. Basically, those initially correct choices were already habits. By the end of the second week, you found that your day went by quite smoothly, and you were now certain that you had made the right career move. By this time, the vast majority of your daily activities were habit, and you essentially no longer had to think about them.

Your mind was relieved to have been saved the burden of having to rethink every option in your daily activities, and all was at peace! One of the attractive consequences of this was that you had a lot more energy at the end of the day.

What happens when you are asked to reshuffle those options and to come up with a new way of doing something—or to find a different approach? Your mind resists the change and causes you to say things like "That won't work" or "We can't possibly handle that within the constraints of this department." Valid objections? Possibly, but not very likely. You are just too lazy at this point to entertain change. If this request for change had come during your first week at the job, you would have welcomed it. At that point you hadn't firmly developed your habits yet, and you were still flexible.

While we might feel that we are the exception, and habits do not control our day, Peter Drucker suggests this is not likely to be the case. He recently observed that almost 80% of the activities in which managers engage are selected out of habit, rather than by intelligent choice.

A Definition of a "Creative Idea"

A creative idea will be defined as any idea that offers a uniquely beneficial solution to the problem at hand.

Surprisingly, one of the reasons that there has been so little research on creativity is that we have yet to come up with a universally applicable definition of it. This may come as a surprise to you, because I suspect that you have a definition that suits your needs just fine. Let me explain why there is a problem in trying to come up with a definition of creativity.

Let's assume that I have been working at a firm for ten years. During this time, I notice that a machine this firm uses is employed not only to perform its original task, but has also been modestly modified to perform a second, different task.

Now assume I have been offered a new job with another firm, and I accept. Soon after beginning with this new firm, I find the same piece of machinery, performing its intended task. It has not, however, been modified to perform the additional task that my former employer had discovered. I suggest to my current employer that the machine can be modified to perform this second task. It is modified to my specifications, and my career is enhanced by my "creative" suggestion.

Was this a creative idea?

The situation gets even muddier when you go a step further. Let's say that I have been in marketing with a toothpaste company for a number of years. In the toothpaste industry we have followed a particular method of advertising. I leave that company and join a firm that markets safety razors. I combine the techniques that I was familiar with in the toothpaste company with those of the razor firm to come up with a unique advertising approach.

Is this a truly creative contribution to my new employer?

The fact is that there is no definition of a truly creative idea that is accepted everywhere. The dictionary says creative input is "showing artistic or intellectual inventiveness." This isn't very helpful. Does inventiveness have to be totally unique to qualify, or is it possible to borrow ideas from existing sources?

While we all would like to generate totally unique ideas, this isn't necessary to meet our needs. Frankly, we don't care where a good idea comes from. We'd be delighted to come up with any unique (for us) idea that provided a solution to a problem we were working on. If the solution met our criterion of being a unique solution to a problem, we wouldn't care where it originated. The idea would be accepted here as creative.

This approach is clearly not hedging on the issue of generating creative ideas. In most cases, ships of innovation have found ports friendlier than their home port. One of the major complaints of inventors in America is the attitude of "not invented here" exhibited by some manufacturers. Their attitude basically says, "if we didn't develop the product, we're not interested."

One of the most recognizably creative people of our age was Thomas Edison, who holds over a thousand patents. It may surprise you to know that his strength was not in innovation, but in accommodation. Thomas Edison's greatest skill was in taking ideas from other inventors and modifying them to add to their practicality, and then in applying for new patents based upon these improvements. This doesn't deny his achievements, nor should it deny ours.

Any idea that is unique and can make a beneficial contribution will meet our definition of a creative idea, no matter its source.

The Creative Stereotype

While basic intelligence helps in anything we do as professionals, we don't need to be brilliant to be creative.

One of the mental habits we develop over time is the tendency to stereotype people. Like all habits, this is a justifiable, if unfair, tendency. The value of this habit is that it saves us the labor of trying constantly to reassess who everyone is. In the back of our minds we have categories representing every type of person we have ever met. There is a category for cool, charming, bright, and professional, as well as many others.

Within a comparatively short period of time after meeting people, we try to put them into one of these categories. The next time we meet them, we don't have to reassess their places in our scheme of things. We simply say, "Oh, yes, there is the charming Mr. Harris" and dismiss the fact that the charming Mr. Harris is currently acting like an idiot.

Our ability to stereotype is enhanced once we discover a person's profession. It isn't difficult to conjure in our mind what a used car salesman, football player, and accountant are supposed to look like. What about a creative person? What does she look like? Does she eat quiche? Gratefully, some of the stereotypes we have developed for the creative person are false.

There has been a great deal of research that has attempted to relate creativity to intelligence. This is a concern to me. If we aren't geniuses, are we wasting our time trying to be creative? Research has come up with two pieces of information that should make us more comfortable. It indicates that a person with an I.Q. of between 60 and 80 will have a hard time generating creative ideas. This can't come as a genuine shock, as people in this I.Q. range have problems with many things, in addition to creativity.

We aren't really worried about the low end of the I.Q. scale, but how about the top? Do we need a 160 I.Q. to perform well in this area? The interesting fact here is that there may be a negative correlation between high I.Q. and creative abilities. The chances are that an intelligent person is deliberately not creative. If you think about it, there is a good reason for this.

From the time the very bright individual entered school and, chances are, before that time as well, he garnered attention by providing the "right" answer to questions. He soon found that he continued to receive positive attention as long as he was able to provide correct answers.

As a bright individual matures, he finds that providing correct answers requires taking a stand on issues in advance of his peers. Having taken this stand, he must then defend it. And he does, with great skill. However, while he is providing the defense for the stance that he has adopted, other, less certain individuals are looking for new options that might work better. In other words, bright individuals are so good at defending their positions that they frequently don't develop the skills necessary to think more flexibly—the very skills that we are going to learn in these chapters.

This book is written for people like us, normal individuals possessed with normal intelligence, who want to learn to think more creatively. If you are among the brightest, welcome aboard. If not, you suffer no disadvantage. If you are able to learn, you can hone your creative skills!

The Creative Climate in the United States

People in America tend to relate creativity to commercial success more than people do in other countries.

Among the many peculiarities of living in the United States is our unique position toward creative thinking. In other countries of the world, the foundations of creativity are found in the arts. An author is considered creative, a painter is considered creative, as is a musician. Public education, if it teaches creativity at all, does so from the perspective of the arts, not commerce.

Unlike many nations, the United States doesn't have a thousand years of philosophy in its history. Nor do we have a thousand years of music or literature to relate to. Rather, the United States is a pragmatic, practical country. As you would expect from such a country, our creative idols have mostly been in the field of commerce. These creative people have applied their skills to advance this country to its current position as the world's largest, most fertile economy. Included are such familiar names as Henry Ford, Thomas Edison, Eli Whitney and Steve Jobs.

You might reasonably ask, "What difference does it make if we emulate artists or industrialists, as long as the result is creative output?" Unfortunately, it ends up making a significant difference.

If I am to become a creative author, I will do so through the use of language, the plot and the message. My attempt, then, is to try to modify creatively that which has been done, but in a recognizably superior way. I know that to succeed as an author, I must necessarily be creative.

This natural progression is muddied substantially in my attempts to emulate a successful industrialist. What is it that I emulate when I try to copy the pattern of a successful business person? The money! I see that person as successful, and the measure of this success is the money that she has been able to generate for herself. So, quite logically, I strike out to be rich. In doing this, however, I completely overlook the fact that my idol is rich first because she is creative. I don't pursue the proper path in following her success. This goes a long way toward explaining why so many start-up businesses fail in their first few years of operation. They are pursuing the wrong objective. They look to create wealth, when they should be looking to innovate first.

Where Creativity Fits in Our Current Thinking

Your ability to think creatively will help you generate new solutions to problems, as you would expect. Another, more subtle, benefit of creative thinking is the increased skill you will develop in finding opportunities to think more creatively.

In our effort to reach decisions, we generally follow a predictable pattern. The steps we use are the same in all cases. These steps can in many ways be aided by our ability to think more creatively.

The first step is the awareness that a problem exists. Basically, we become aware of a problem in one of two ways: when something doesn't happen that we expect to happen or when something does happen that we didn't expect.

Another key step in our problem solving sequence is that of generating alternative solutions to solve the problem.

Whether or not you have ever laid out these steps, this is basically the way that we arrive at solutions to our problems. What I'd like to do is give you some idea of where creativity fits into this sequence of steps. Surprisingly, the above step that is most aided by creativity is the first one, that of recognizing that a problem exists. We tend not to see opportunities for improvement because we have been taught the principle that, "If it ain't broke, don't fix it."

Imagine the number of opportunities we have had to improve things—opportunities lost because we saw nothing was broken. If we feel that nothing is broken, then we see no need for improvement. This is simply not true.

Consider the number of products that you and I take for granted which were developed simply because they were better and not because what existed "was broke." Into this category we have to include the automobile, although the horse wasn't "broke"; the radio and television, although our ability to entertain ourselves wasn't "broke"; and the telephone, although our ability to communicate directly wasn't "broke."

If the developers of these significant new products had waited until what existed at the time finally "broke," we would have had none of these products. I believe that the principle of "if it ain't broke, don't fix it" has cost us hundreds, maybe thousands, of new and significant products. The more quickly we ignore that advice the better off we'll be.

In the second step described above, that of generating alternative solutions, we also will use our creative abilities. Logically, we can select our solution only from a list of alternatives we have developed. Therefore, the ability to list numerous options is very important.

What Happens During a Creative Insight

Creative insights tend not to be random. Their occurrences show some patterns.

There is research available that indicates what happens to people when they come up with a creative idea. One of the images frequently identified with a creative idea is defined best as a "thunderbolt." Reading about how people come up with creative ideas, you frequently see this event as a sudden insight on their part or a "thunderbolt." They can't explain how it happened, it simply came to them.

While this testimony is honest, it is not at all accurate. There are a series of things that happen prior to this revelation. The ideas didn't just come out of the air, they have some characteristics in common. Some of these characteristics include the following:

- The idea usually goes against a prior belief.
- There is always a lot of work involved. When you come up with a significant idea, you typically have spent a number of hours doing so. It may not seem that way because you were absorbed in the project and lost track of time. But the result was still the same: you had invested many hours into it before the idea came to you.
- The idea does not come when you are working on it. Instead it comes during a time of relaxation.

As a student at Michigan State University, I remember being introduced to this fact during an advertising class. The instructor had done an excellent job of explaining the technical aspects of advertising, but had apparently ignored the more elusive creative aspects of that profession. This was a major omission, as creativity is the core of successful advertising. To compensate for the void, our professor had invited an executive from a Detroit advertising agency to lecture to our class on how to generate creative advertising ideas.

His suggestion was to let ideas "ferment" by absorbing as much information as possible on the advertising campaign that you wanted to create, and then play a game of golf. Or take in a movie. Or work on a hobby. He said that the idea for the campaign would simply come to you during the relaxation or "fermentation" time.

I felt at the time that this was a bit weak-kneed for a profession as supposedly fast-paced as advertising, but his advice fits perfectly with what we now know about how the creative process works. Ideas won't come to us while we are concentrating on them; we need to set them aside for a while to let them develop.

Your Creative Handicaps

Each of us shares common beliefs that limit our ability to generate innovative ideas.

Because you have purchased this book, it is safe to assume some things concerning your outlook on life. First, you would like to think more creatively, for that is the purpose of this verbal missile. Second, you aren't afraid to make a modest investment in your future if you think there will be a payoff.

You also depend heavily on your education and experience to improve your life. This assumption isn't based upon your purchase of this book; it is based on the fact that each of us depends on our experience and education to better our circumstances.

This is unfortunate, for in the area of innovative thinking, relying primarily on your education and experience will invariably let you down.

Your Search for "One Right Answer"

Your academic training unwittingly teaches you to look for only one solution to every problem or situation.

From the time you started in school, either in kindergarten or the first grade, you were indoctrinated with the notion that there is always one right answer to every question. When you were able to provide that one right answer, you were rewarded with advancement to the next grade and received positive reports from the school to your parents. If you failed to provide it, you suffered the humiliation of falling behind your peers and whatever indignities your parents chose to heap on you.

While the concept of "One Right Answer" was never explained to you in these terms, it certainly was one you grew to understand early on. Not only did you understand it, but after 12 years of having it subtly drilled into your head, the concept became an integral part of the way you approached life. Which was no big deal—until you became an adult.

Imagine now that you have graduated from school and are interviewing for your first job. Your interviewer asks if you can perform a particular task. You answer that you can, which is only partially accurate. What you should more honestly say is that you have found "One Right Way" to perform that task. Not one of several ways, not a way that could be improved and modified; but the "One Right Way."

Your interviewer is so impressed that you get the job. Now, as an employee, you learn to do a lot of other jobs as well. You feel after a few years that it is time to make a career move, so you begin interviewing again. This time you are in a much stronger position, as you can do a number of jobs in addition to the one you could do before your career began, and you don't hesitate to tell your interviewer as much.

You get the new job. Now your experience hasn't made you a fool. You know that you are being hired for this new job not because the company wants to train you, but because they expect results immediately. Even if you had a tendency to take risks, you are less inclined to do so at this time. Nosirree, you're going to stick with what you know.

The "One Right Way" to do every job you have to handle becomes your bible, and you will brook no variation.

Your education subtly taught you to look for "One Right Answer," and that tendency has carried over into your career as well—interpreted now as the "One Right Way." Your education has dulled your creative tendencies and become your enemy in situations requiring creativity.

If there is only one way to do everything, why then are there so many ways to enclose a bottle (screw lid, cork, pressure cap, etc.)?

The Stifling Effects of Our Work Experience

Like our education, our work experience tends to stifle our innovative abilities.

Your work experience further refines the limitations initiated by your education. It does so by teaching you that "the ultimately correct answer to any problem comes from equally correct suggestions."

This advice has been written nowhere, nor was it passed on to us by a thoughtful mentor. It is simply something we have been led to believe and apply every day. What this teaches us is that fundamentally incorrect suggestions have no value in creative problem-solving process. This is false. Frequently, fundamentally incorrect suggestions serve as a "trigger" for other, more applicable and unique solutions.

We will see a clear example of this at the end of the present chapter.

What is the Benefit of Your Education and Experience?

Our education and professional experience provide the tools needed to think more creatively. However, we need to learn to use them to expand our thinking, rather than let them do the thinking for us.

I was conducting an innovation workshop for a group of business professionals in Ohio a few years ago, and one of the participants asked me if I meant to say that Albert Einstein could have developed the theory of relativity without his education and experience. No, of course I didn't mean that. But Albert Einstein had a unique ability that we intend to develop in the pages of this book—that of *parlaying his education and experience* into creative insights, rather than letting those two factors limit his creativity. By the time we finish this book, you will learn how to do so as well.

Interestingly, Albert Einstein himself referred to his creative abilities in a way that should help us understand how he perceived their importance. Einstein said:

"In reviewing the way that I think and use my mind, I have greater regard for my ability to fantasize than I do for my ability to absorb absolute information."

I wonder how many physicists would make that same statement, but then I wonder how many Albert Einsteins there are in this world.

The Schedule for Increasing Our Creative Output

To develop our innovative abilities, we will pursue a series of steps that will force us to see things in a more mentally flexible manner.

First we will look at the things that restrict our creativity. There is a body of research that indicates that children are naturally creative. The same research indicates that by the time we reach the age of 40, we are about two percent as creative as we were as a child. What happened? Can this be reversed? Can we bring back the creativity we once had? There are things we can do, and we'll cover these in the next chapter.

Next, we will measure our creative output. There is an old phrase that says, "If you want a good idea, get lots of ideas." That is the bylaw we will adhere to in this book. We'll show you a technique for reliably measuring your creative output. This is a technique you can use yourself in a few minutes each day. Not only will using the technique measure your output of creative ideas, but it will also show you what you need to do to increase your score!

Lastly, we will show you several specific techniques for increasing your creative output. These aren't difficult concepts to grasp. Instead they are easy tools that will broaden your insights, the same insights that you have permitted to be narrowed over the years. These techniques have been chosen from the many available for one simple reason: they can be taught the same way you and I have been taught everything we know. That is, through practice and repetition. We know that if we practice these tools enough, we will become more creative.

Applications of Creative Thinking

Creative applications are around us every day. In reviewing them, we can see the potential of innovative logic.

To help you understand how the concept of creative application works in a practical setting, I'd like to give you a couple of examples.

The first of these examples comes to us from ancient

history, the other from a personal experience of mine.

One of the major military conflicts in history was the Persian War, fought by the Athenians and the Greeks. At one particular juncture of this war, it became apparent that the Persians were in a position to win the war.

In Greece, as in most ancient cultures, oracles were used to assist in running the country and the military. It was the responsibility of the oracle to tell the leaders what to do during stressful times. It was also customary during these times to behead the bearers of bad news. The oracles, to maintain their longevity, would give advice that required substantial interpretation. By so doing, they could correctly claim always to be right, and further insist that any misfortune that befell the followers of their advice was a function of misinterpretation.

The Greek leaders approached the oracle and asked his counsel. After being told of the dilemma facing the Greek nation, the oracle said, "Trust the wooden wall." This advice certainly met the criteria of ambiguity, as no one could agree as to what the advice meant. Since the Acropolis was at that time surrounded by a wooden wall, some observers felt that the oracle meant for them to retreat to the Acropolis and defend their country from there. Other observers thought that they should run to their boats and leave their city to the Persians.

The prevailing logic suggested that the advice encouraged them to engage the Persians at sea, which is what they did, and they met with complete military success. If we review this story, it doesn't take any real genius to confirm the fact that the oracle's advice was much too vague to be of any real value. The value of the advice, it seems, comes from forcing the listener to try to apply it. Given this thread of information, the listeners were forced to think on their own, whether or not they wanted to.

To use the information, the listeners had to rethink

how it could apply to their situation. There is reason to suspect that the successful military campaign that followed the oracle's counsel was more a result of the thinking that followed the advice than the advice itself.

The second example comes from an experience with a long-time friend. I cling firmly to the theory that we learn information too soon. That is, we learn a piece of information, have no place to use it, and therefore forget it. Many years later, we relearn that same piece of information but, because we're now able to use it, the information is retained and becomes part of our bank of working knowledge.

Such was the case in this example, when my friend gave me some valuable insights into creativity, and I forgot them until many years later.

Jim had been my friend since high school. From the first time we met I had great regard for his ability to "get it done." Although the reasons for my admiration in school weren't always based on noble causes, Jim had leveraged his substantial skills throughout his professional career, and predictably had enjoyed great success. As we both travel a great deal, there were a number of years when our chats were all held in airports, where one or the other of us was waiting to fly to some business related destination.

At the time this story took place, Jim was the production vice president of a medium sized firm in the San Francisco area. What this firm was could best be described as a "high tech job shop." This firm manufactured one-of-a-kind circuit boards. The drawings for the circuit boards would be provided by the customer. Each was then transferred to a microfiche, and the microfiche taken to the production area.

Production was handled exclusively by women, based on the theory that their manual dexterity was superior to men's (and, I suppose, based also on their lower wage requirements). Each of the several dozen women were surrounded by bins of parts necessary to build circuit boards. The microfiche of the needed board would flash on a screen in front of their position, and they would begin the tedious task of building the circuit board. As this firm specialized in one-of-a-kind boards, each board would present new challenges for the assemblers. There were no duplicates and, therefore, no learning curve.

As you might imagine, these women were highly skilled, and typically took several months of training, up to eighteen in fact, before they were sufficiently proficient to net the company any profit. The problem, as explained to me by my friend, was that once the women became proficient in their jobs, they also experienced a substantial increase in their marketability. Many chose to take advantage of this windfall and moved on to other firms.

In explaining how the firm handled this dilemma of expensive employee turnover, Jim gave me valuable insights into how creativity plays an important role in our daily lives. In hopes that you see the connection more quickly than I did, I will relay the conclusion of this story to you.

As an officer of the company, Jim served on the board of directors. At one board meeting, the problem of turnover in the production area was discussed. While the other members of the board reviewed the pros and cons of each alternative solution, Jim sat and thought to himself, "The problem of employee turnover can be most simply stated as people walking out of the plant. If we tied their legs together, they wouldn't be able to walk out, and our turnover problems would be solved."

Apparently secure in his future with this firm, Jim passed on to the other board members his simplified logic. His "suggestion" raised some eyebrows and a few nervous twitters from all but one of those present. The human resource director, new to the firm, sat quietly for a few moments. Then, interrupting the conversation which had moved on to supposedly more fertile territory, he offered his interpretation of what Jim had suggested. "You know," he began, "at my former firm, we frequently hired people with disabilities if they had the capacity to do the job. We found that they were more loyal, easier to train, less likely to suffer from Monday morning flu, rarely late, and virtually never absent. They were, in fact, a clearly superior employee!"

The idea was met with a respectful silence, as each member of the board mulled over the risk that they might be exposed to by agreeing with an idea that had such a shaky foundation. Jim, whose responsibilities included the production area, was the first to voice approval, and he was soon followed by others.

From then on, any new hires were drawn from the available pool of people with disabilities, male and female. The results were a pleasant surprise, even for Jim and the human resource director. Within two years the turnover had dropped from 40% per year to less than 5%, a remarkable level in this highly volatile industry.

The information that Jim gave me in that story relates to two principles that we will use in chapters to come. The first of these is the technique of "Redefinition." When Jim first considered this situation, his approach was based upon changing the definition of the problem that he was reviewing. If you recall, he suggested that the problem was one of people walking out of the plant; this is a simple redefinition of the problem as originally understood.

The second technique which Jim introduced to me that day was the use of "Off-Road Thinking." This is more a philosophy than a technique, as it gives the thinker permission to think in other than straight lines, as we all are prone to do. His offer to tie his employees' legs together was clearly not a product of the logic we use every day. It was, however, the logic that provided the needed solution. "Off-Road Thinking" is something else we'll cover in future chapters.

Jim's experience also shows us that the idea that "the ultimately correct solution will come from equally correct suggestions" is also false. His idea of tying employees' legs together was clearly flawed, but it provided the basis for the ultimately correct idea. This issue was briefly mentioned earlier in this chapter.

Mind Expansion Exercises

1. What "priors" affect your thinking in:

   - Developing ways to improve our political system?
   - Designing a house?
   - Solving the problem of heavy traffic on our city streets?
   - Generating a climate of positive reinforcement in your family?
   - Reducing the bureaucracy where you work?

2. List the habits you have developed at home and at work. How do these habits restrict your creativity?

For potential approaches to the above problems, refer to the "Possibilities" section at the end of this book.

Chapter Two:

Mind Sets That Limit Our Creativity

SUMMARY OF CHAPTER ONE:

1. Our prior experiences tend to set the tone for our future patterns of thinking. By accepting our history as the basis for new ideas, we are basically suggesting that the future is just an extrapolation of the past. This is not true.
2. Habits we develop in our personal and professional lives serve to lull us into accepting the status quo. When we are doing things by habit, we aren't thinking.
3. Our education and experience, while invaluable tools for personal development, subtly teach us lessons that limit our search for new approaches.
4. A creative idea is any idea that is uniquely beneficial, regardless of its source.
5. Creativity does not require a high level of intelligence. As a matter of fact, personal brilliance may well work against our creative efforts.
6. In addition to helping us generate more alternative solutions to problems, enhanced creative abilities also help us see the opportunity for constructive change.
7. Creative insights are not random events. They normally follow when some predictable steps are executed.

OBJECTIVES OF CHAPTER TWO:

1. To help direct our work throughout this book, we will discuss some relevant problems or opportunities associated with creativity, and discuss solutions to these problems.
2. To help identify our personal barriers to creativity, we will identify five distinct types of barriers.
3. To understand the principle of "acceptable mediocrity."

Have you ever noticed that you are much better at solving your neighbor's problems than you are at solving your own?

This is especially true in business consulting. Clients come to their consultant and explain a business problem that they are dealing with. After a number of questions and extended conversation, the consultant offers the solution which he feels will be best.

In some cases, the only advantage the consultant has in solving the problem is that of an outsider's perspective. The client's judgment is muddied by conflicting personalities, imagined agenda, and information that is superfluous to the situation. In other words, the client has too much experience and education in that issue to review it objectively.

A consultant friend provided me with an example of this not long ago. He was speaking with a client who was in food processing. The client was complaining that the profits were so low in her industry that she found it difficult to invest in new equipment.

After some questions, the client advised that the only time the company had been truly profitable was when it successfully introduced a new product into the market. This nugget of information had been buried in a conversation that consumed over two hours and covered every facet of her business.

The consultant took his client's information and suggested that she plan two new product introductions per year. This pace would keep awareness of her brand high in the marketplace, keep competition off stride, and provide her with at least two profitable products each year.

Her initial reaction was that the suggestion was impossible, and in defending her position, she listed reasons why it would be difficult. Her defense was based on information not directly relevant to the situation.

It is natural for us to look at people in authority—our parents, bosses, teachers—and identify them as rigid or unimaginative when they reject our ideas. Have you ever considered that in some situations you are as unyielding as they are? Normally, in defense of our immovable position, we complain that the person who has the audacity to suggest we change "simply doesn't have the facts." Those "facts" are the same ones our parents, bosses, and teachers had when they rejected our ideas.

Strangely, while "facts" provide the security of letting us believe that we are right on a particular issue, they also thwart our creativity when in the hands of others. Basically, if you take a close look at it, the misuse of "facts" is the root of much rigid thinking. People hide behind the information they have, rather than letting this information lead to brighter and better solutions.

The Problems We Wish to Deal With

To assure that our progress in learning to think creatively is not just an intellectual exercise, we will list problems or situations we would like to provide beneficial solutions for. We will use the techniques contained in this book to provide those solutions.

If it's easier to work on problems that aren't relevant to us, it makes sense to begin practicing on these types of problems. To be sure, however, that we eventually do develop solutions that are meaningful to us, pause for a moment and list in the space below at least three problems or situations for which you would like to find more creative solutions. These problems can be personal, professional, family, new inventions or anything else you would like. Be sure to list them, however, as they will be referred to frequently as we go through this book.

1.__________________________________
2.__________________________________
3.__________________________________

As you learn to use the techniques for thinking more creatively, you will want to go back to the problems listed above and attempt to develop solutions for them.

The Five Types of Barriers to Creativity

Habit, education, and experience all restrain our creativity if we let them. Below are the five categories of barriers they create.

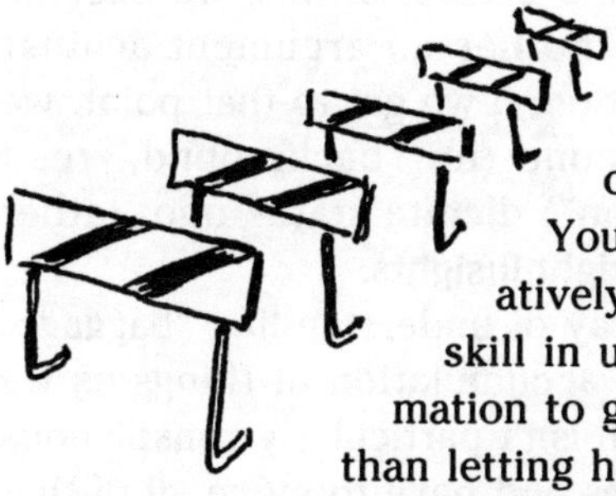

The most significant restraint to your creativity is your reliance on historical information. Your ability to think more creatively is dependent upon your skill in using this historical information to generate new ideas, rather than letting historical information limit your mental flexibility.

In the field of psychology, when treating certain types of neurosis, an analyst will attempt to help a patient see and understand the patient's logic. The purpose of this exercise is to demonstrate that if we can see how our thinking is affected, then we can change it to a more desirable pattern. The next section is based on the same logic. If you and I can see how our creativity is limited, we can learn to overcome these limits.

Each of the following barriers is a result of our habits, education and experience—when we don't use them to expand our ability to think. As we discussed before, they are a result of lazy thinking.

The field of psychology also provides a term that best

describes our tendency to improperly use our education and experience. That term is "baggage." "Baggage" is used in reference to the impact that former relationships have on current relationships. For instance, if a relationship between marriage partners is discontinued, our experience of that relationship continues to have an impact on future relationships that is far out of proportion to its true applicability. This baggage serves to limit our flexibility in future interactions with other people.

These barriers serve to do exactly the same thing in terms of our creativity. The more experience we have, the more restraints or "baggage" we carry with us to the next experience. After some period of time, we become the dreaded nay-sayer who has an argument against every new idea or innovation. If we get to that point, we will have let our background (for "background," read "experience and education") dictate status quo, rather than using it to develop bright insights.

Another more visual way of understanding "baggage" is to look at our gradual accumulation of things as we mature. This accumulation isn't particularly conspicuous until we change residences and have to move all of that stuff. In my career, I have moved 17 times, and the quantity of my baggage (or things) has increased geometrically. When I left college for my first job, I rented the smallest trailer I could find, and asked for a discount because only half of it was occupied.

Some two years later, a new job necessitated a move out of town, and the vehicle of choice was a cargo van, borrowed from a friend. My last move was across town, and it required four trips in the biggest truck that the rental firm offered. I had obviously acquired a lot of baggage and, although it provided for my creature comforts, it had begun to limit my flexibility. Career baggage does the same thing, and the only way you can prevent it from happening is to make a conscious effort not to let the baggage pile up.

We sometimes can see the results of this type of "baggage-inspired" logic in observing the way other people think. Two friends are discussing a new car purchase one of them is about to make. The non-purchasing party to the conversation advises the other to avoid four cylinder engines at all cost. Ruling out four cylinder vehicles reduced by one-half the number of automobiles that the purchaser can choose. Not only this, but it tends to rule out the vehicles that have the best gasoline mileage—a criteria of the prospective buyer.

As the conversation continues, it comes out that the negativity towards four cylinder engines is based on a bad experience suffered 15 years earlier with one of the first domestically-built compact cars. The reputation of that particular car was, in fact, terrible, but the bias expressed is no longer appropriate, as that manufacturer has corrected the reliability problems and now makes very dependable cars. The baggage introduced by the speaker is out of date, incorrect and misleading, even though he continues to carry and spread it. He hasn't rethought his position, and most likely won't.

1. The Guiding Principle

The first barrier is the "guiding principle." A guiding principle is an idea that we accept, absolutely and completely. We are so sure of the idea's validity that we never question or review its applicability. We never write it down, never challenge it, never even mention it. It has simply become part of our value system. Just like the person who won't go near a four cylinder engine, we will take no new input on this issue.

As much as we rely on a guiding principle, this idea sometimes bars our ability to see useful information, or distorts our ability to use that information.

Suppose we are approached by people who want to open a new grocery store. They suggest that since our profession is marketing, we surely must be qualified to do the floor plan for their new store. We agree with this notion and consent to lay out the new store.

With all our years in marketing we have learned, if nothing else, that the customer must be placed first in the company pecking order if a profit is to be earned. This idea, now a "guiding principle" after all the years of loyal adherence on our part, would likely be reflected in our floor plan. The aisles would be wide, customers would have easy access throughout the store, the entire layout would be a celebration of our doctrine of "customer first."

Now imagine, with all this emphasis on customer convenience, where would you likely find the milk? After all, it is almost an impulse item, likely to be purchased alone and spontaneously. Logically, it should be placed in the front of the store, near the check-out lines, right?

Where do you actually find the milk? As far away from the entrance and exit as the store management can place it without violating the property lines. Is our "guiding principle" wrong? Is placing the customer first not a priority of the store? In this case, our guiding principle was not as appropriate to the situation as was the guiding principle of the company accountant. The thinking of the accountant was that if you could use the appeal of milk to draw the customers past the higher margin merchandise, there was a better chance that you would realize additional sales. Regrettably, he was right.

Our guiding principle isn't necessarily wrong, it is just less appropriate. If we had taken the time to write this guiding principle down, we might well have reached the conclusion that it is less relevant in this situation. But we didn't write it down, or challenge its validity. We simply followed it obediently into whatever mischief it had for us.

The danger to us is not that we have guiding principles, but that we never deliberately reassess their usefulness. By not doing so, we're condemned to rigid thinking. It is the capacity to rethink that we need to develop.

2. The Historical Factor

The second form of barrier is the "historical factor." A historical factor is different than a guiding principle primarily in terms of numbers and strength. Whereas we generally have only one guiding principle in each situation, we have any number of historical factors in the same situation. In addition, the depth of commitment is much stronger to the guiding principle than it is to the historical factor. The similarities between a guiding principle and a historical factor are found in their impact on your idea flexibility; that is, they both stifle it.

An example of a historical factor might help you spot them in your thinking process. For a period of time, a friend worked in the marketing department of a relatively large firm. While this firm was large, it was far from the largest in the industry. As a result, she had to use the firm's marketing dollars much more carefully than did her competitors. For each promotional expense, she constantly tried to get multiple benefits. It was particularly attractive to spend advertising dollars that also proved to be newsworthy as well. This was fairly difficult, as she had to have a message for the customer that the press found interesting enough to print as a news item.

This happy circumstance would occur whenever the firm could concentrate its advertising into a brief period of time, secure substantial sales gains over the prior year, and then issue a press release featuring its successes. The difficulty in this setup was the rate schedules used by the advertising media. All sales results in this industry were released in ten day periods, not in weeks or months. Contrarily, all of the advertising media offered daily, weekly, and monthly rates. Nothing was available in ten day periods.

It was decided that there was no reason that newspapers, TV, and radio couldn't offer a rate for ten days that was more attractive than the weekly rate. After all, logic told her, her firm was talking about running ads a longer period of time so they should get the benefit of a lower rate.

While this might sound reasonable, the media found it less so. Initially she tried to talk to the media representatives over the telephone, but results were so dismal, she started making direct contact. The reaction was the same everywhere, "We don't offer a ten day rate." She would advise them that she was aware of that. If they had such a rate, she wouldn't be asking for it!

The historical factor in this case was the experience in the media of never before providing a ten day rate for advertising space that was more attractive than a seven day rate. There was no reason not to offer the new rate; it certainly made sense. The pull of historical precedent was so strong that the suggestion wouldn't even be considered. Finally, a publisher was contacted and the situation explained to him. He was frankly stunned that his staff had so little imagination, and didn't hesitate to say so. She quickly got her rate concession from all of the media departments she approached after the first one agreed.

In this case, the historical factor was precedent. It was sufficiently strong to prevent any reconsiderations, no matter how logical they seemed.

To give another example of how a historical factor may limit your thinking, take a look at the situation to the right.

There are four volumes of Shakespeare's collected works on the shelf. The pages of each volume

volume are exactly 2" thick. The covers are each $^1/_6$" thick. The bookworm started eating at page 1 of volume I and it ate through to the last page of volume IV. What is the distance the bookworm covered?

answer: ____________

Review the instructions again. They ask you to start from page one of Volume I. Where is page one of Volume I? On the far right hand side of the book, right? If the bookworm is heading for Volume II, he doesn't eat any of the pages of Volume I, he eats only the back cover. Similarly, the bookworm eats none of the pages of Volume IV to get to the last page of that volume.

The correct distance is five inches. Our thinking was tethered by the instruction, "He begins at page one of Volume I and eats through to the last page of Volume IV." We logically assumed that all pages would be eaten. After a second look, we now see that the way the volumes were lined up on the shelf, the pages of Volume I would be untouched. You read, but didn't apply the information to the situation.

3. Limited Options

The third type of barrier is "limited options." Whenever you are given a fixed number of alternative responses, you are being subjected to the limited option effect. We feel, because we're asked to consider more than one alternative, that we're being given the chance to be creative. This is not the case. All of the thinking that goes into the situation has already been done by the time we are consulted.

If someone asks us to pick a choice from six options, we aren't being given the right to think creatively because the directions have already been determined. We tend to believe we have flexibility in that situation, but we don't. The framework has been laid out for us.

Many years ago a friend worked for an individual for whom he had great regard. My friend thought that his boss was about as professional as anyone he had worked with before, and he learned a great deal from him.

My friend's firm had been given three proposals for a sales promotion campaign by its advertising agency. His boss called him into his office and asked him to evaluate each of the proposed campaigns and make a recommendation. Flushed with power, he swaggered back into his office to wax critical.

He was into his second hour of evaluation before he realized that each proposal was virtually identical to the next. All would cost the company about the same, and all provided roughly the same benefit. More importantly, since the company was short-staffed, none of them took more of internal staff time than the other. Initially, he wasn't quite sure how to handle it. After all, he didn't want to appear wishy-washy in what could be his hour of triumph. By the same token, he wasn't about to recommend a program he couldn't see as clearly superior.

It occurred to him that the options from which he had been asked to choose had already been chosen. As we mentioned above, the insidious part of this was that my friend believed he had been given the right to be creative, but just the opposite was true. Such is the impact of limited option thinking.

He could have flipped a coin or thrown darts and made an equally good decision. The predetermined options among which we are asked to choose are limiting factors, not contributors to our mental flexibility.

4. Boundaries

Our mental flexibility is also limited by what I call "boundaries." Perhaps the simplest way to show you this barrier is by example. Read the instructions on the following page and solve the problem.

Draw four straight lines through these nine dots without lifting or retracing your pen.

Every "right thinking" adult takes a look at that problem and assumes that the boundary within which the problem must be solved is defined by the square formed by the dots. The instructions don't indicate or imply that, but we assume it anyway. We feel that any solution must fit within those nine dots. That's wrong! Nobody told us that. Had we written down the restraint that "the solution must fit within the dots," we could see that it, in fact, wasn't supportable. The problem is that we never wrote it down, so we weren't in a position to challenge it. The correct solution is shown below. Note that the lines travel well beyond the perimeter of the nine dots.

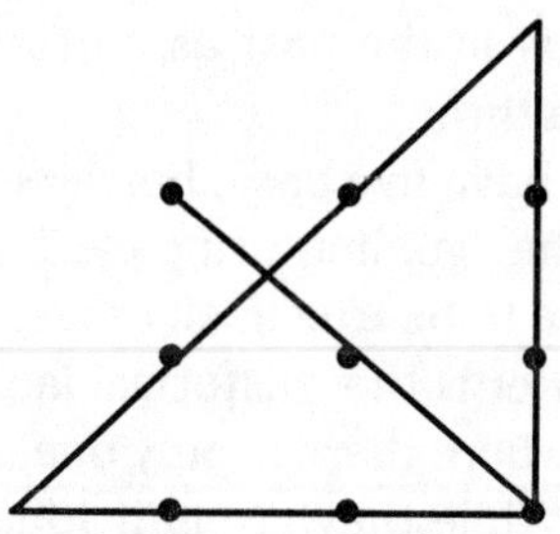

Boundaries tend to be numeric. In business, a common boundary is the budget, where the exact number of dollars available to fix a problem has been defined. Within every company there is a belief that any solution will have to fit within the dollar restraints established by the budget.

Another boundary is the notion that the solution to any business problem will have to come from the current staff. This is a situation where the restraint on the number of people available to solve a problem is never written down, never challenged. If it were, it would be obvious that it was inappropriate. The number of people was never dictated, but this numeric restraint is taken for granted.

5. Assumptions

Our last barrier is "assumptions." Assumptions are the starting point of all thinking. While we're warned constantly not to assume anything, it is our reasonable assumptions that make us valuable in our work. Once we develop experience, our assumptions form the framework of our entire decision-making process. We have to assume; if we didn't, we'd have to constantly re-substantiate everything in our work. Those assumptions become a large share of what we use in our thinking.

The problem is that over a long period of time our assumptions become more rigid; we use the assumptions that have served us in the past as a crutch rather than thinking a situation through.

In summary, we have five basic barriers to our creative thinking. First is the "guiding principle." This is a single idea that we believe to be true in all cases.

The second barrier is the "historical factor." Unlike the guiding principle, where there is only one, there are many historical factors. While they are individually less imposing in terms of impact on our creativity, these factors add up to severely restrain our innovativeness.

The third barrier is the "limited options" that people impose on us. Any time we have our options numerically limited we are subconsciously permitting ourselves to be confined in our thinking.

The fourth restraint is referred to as "boundaries." These are typically numeric limits that either are appropriate to a situation, or that we believe are appropriate.

Last are our "assumptions," which form the basis for all of our thinking. If not used carefully, they cause us to think in a much more restricted manner.

Taking Advantage of Your Education and Experience

Properly utilized, your education and experience provide the framework for every creative idea you will ever have. How to take advantage of your background and not permit your experiences to dictate your thinking is the key.

Any predisposition I have about a problem can serve to restrict my thinking. The only way I can isolate the impact that preconceived notions have on my mental flexibility is by writing down everything I know, or believe to be true, about the problem.

The value of learning to create lists of our ideas concerning a problem is clear. As we write down the idea (preconceived notion or belief) we can challenge the applicability of the idea to this situation. The result is that our minds are using prior experiences to see new options, rather than letting these old and perhaps outdated ideas limit our thinking. We are using our experience and education, not hiding behind them.

After we have practiced this technique for several weeks, we will learn how to do it "on our feet." It will become second nature to review everything we know about a situation before we start considering solutions. In looking back at my use of this tool, I compare it to learning long division. As a child, I can recall spending inordinate amounts of time trying to master long division, a skill that seemed to follow none of my previously established norms. Over the months I practiced the techniques, I developed skill in solving long division problems. Without the practice, it never would have happened. Now if I am asked to divide a number into another number, I can do so "on my feet" and give you a good approximation of the correct answer.

Learning to write down everything we know or believe to be true about a problem is exactly the same kind of skill. It goes counter to our natural instincts. The results of using this technique, I assure you, will be every bit as satisfying as was learning long division when you were a child.

Just as you didn't wait for your first test to practice long division, you can't learn this technique under pressure. If you take this technique back to your office and avoid using it until you are forced by circumstances to do so, it won't work for you. You need to practice it first under pressure-free circumstances if you expect to be able to use it under pressure.

The difference between long division and this technique is that this technique is already in your head. All you have to do is write it down and use it.

The trap to avoid is that of trying to identify the category each barrier fits into. We don't care if your list includes all assumptions, all historical factors or all boundaries. The purpose of showing these categories is to trigger different types of restraints in your mind. It is very much like using the words "door" or "gate." If I visualize a gate, I see something that is rectangular, that swings open and shut, and separates one area from another. If I visualize a door, I also see something that is rectangular, swings open and shut, and separates one area from another; but I see something that is very different than a gate.

The five categories of restraints serve exactly the same purpose. They represent different ways of saying essentially the same thing; each is a category of ideas that we believe are true. The benefit of these ideas is that we become more "experienced" and "educated" because we have them. The drawback is that once we have developed the ideas, we don't ever reevaluate them. If the ideas aren't reevaluated, they become restraints to our creativity. Writing each idea down gives us the opportunity to reevaluate them.

Resisting the Pull of "Acceptable Mediocrity"

In our jobs we are unconsciously attracted to performing at a level far below our capabilities. In most of our career, this really is not a problem, but in the area of innovation, it can be doubly destructive.

The phrase "acceptable mediocrity" may be new to you. After hearing the definition, however, you will not only understand what the term means, but you will also be able to attach a co-worker's name to it!

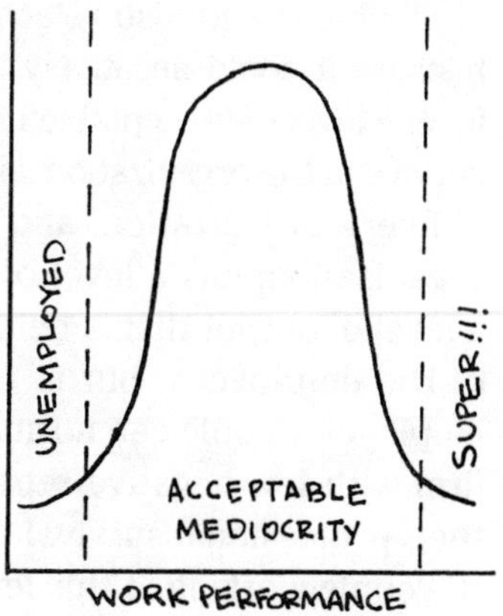

The term "acceptable mediocrity" refers to the level of performance that many people aspire to. How they end up in that position is unfortunate but, in many cases, predictable.

Instinctively, all of us understand at least three levels of performance in our jobs. The first level is most identifiable during our first few months in a new job. During that time we all aspire to verify our employer's confidence in us by performing at the highest level we can.

We work overtime, make many suggestions, and try to be conspicuously diligent. Unfortunately, some organizations fail to recognize our extra efforts, and the rewards we expect to accrue from this output are not forthcoming. Sometimes the fault is ours, expecting too much too soon, or feeling that our work is exceptional when, in fact, it isn't.

Whatever the cause, we soon abandon this first, high-output level of performance as we don't feel the rewards will be there for us.

The second level of performance we are aware of could be referred to ungraciously as "on the street," or unemployed. We know better than to operate long at this low level or we will find ourselves out of a job. We may choose to leave the firm, but it would be much more attractive to leave at a time of our own choosing.

We have rejected a high level of performance due to a lack of feedback; and also rejected a low level of performance because it could negatively affect our career. We then look for the level of "acceptable mediocrity" that will enable us to survive in the organization, and not tax our abilities.

Every organization, and every department within the organization, has a level of "acceptable mediocrity." It is a level of output that is below the capacity of the majority of the employees, but is considered acceptable by the employer. People can normally operate at this level in the firm with few negative repercussions, and little threat to their professional survival.

People working at this level are not prone to make new

suggestions, are not likely to show up early in the morning or work late after regular hours. They volunteer for little, and complain when given new assignments. In other words, their level of inspiration is very low.

As you might suspect, when we, or our coworkers, are operating at a level of "acceptable mediocrity," we are not likely to offer innovative ideas. The problem is seen by the employer as a basic lack of creative ingenuity, but is actually much more serious than that. This level of performance has become a habit, and a very difficult one to break.

Fortunately, people respond positively if given the opportunity to think. Offering the chance to make unique contributions to their work often will pull an employee out of a mediocre performance habit. If we see acceptable mediocrity in ourselves, we need to remember the original enthusiasm we displayed in our jobs, and remember too that the first beneficiary of a uniquely constructive idea is ourselves!

Mind Expansion Exercises

1. Make a list of everything you know, or believe to be true, about dealing with difficult people (remember that this list is actually a list of restraints to your thinking).

   Now challenge each and every one of these "facts." Are they all true in every situation? How many of them do you automatically believe, without ever challenging?

2. Select one of the problems you identified at the beginning of Chapter Two and make a list of everything you know, or believe to be true about that problem.

   Now challenge each of these "facts." Are they all true in this situation? How many of them have you believed without question, yet now find only partially applicable?

For potential approaches to the above problems, refer to the "Possibilities" section at the end of this book.

Chapter Three:

The Beginnings of Innovative Thinking

SUMMARY OF CHAPTER TWO:

1. One of the products of our education and experience is the development of barriers to our creativity. These barriers generally fall into five types: the guiding principle, historical factors, limited options, boundaries, and assumptions.
2. While each of these barriers reduces our creative output, they also represent the core of all the creative ideas we will ever have in the future. That being the case, we must learn how to parlay these barriers into innovative ideas, rather than permit them to dominate our thinking.
3. The development of innovative ideas is demanding, and very difficult to execute by people whose commitment level is low. When our jobs do not push us past mediocrity, we have to provide self-induced motivation to be successful at generating innovative ideas.

OBJECTIVES OF CHAPTER THREE:

1. Since the ability to use our barriers to creativity to generate creative ideas is so important to our progress, in this chapter we provide additional examples of this technique.
2. We will also develop a technique for measuring

our creative output, and learn to use this measuring device to increase our productivity of innovative ideas.

As a result of our education, experience and habits, we tend to develop fixed ideas. These fixed ideas are a saving grace to us under normal circumstances. They enable us to make quick and generally accurate judgments concerning problems we encounter.

For instance, these fixed ideas enable us to promptly decide on disputes between our children, spur of the moment changes in our job, and what we can prepare on short notice for an unexpected guest for dinner.

Despite this obvious benefit, this background and experience betrays us when we're given the opportunity to think creatively. Because "no" is one of the first words we hear as a child, it is a great fall-back word when we are confused. In this situation, we tend to let our education and experience do our thinking for us, and we become the legendary bottleneck that everyone dislikes. We can certainly justify our immobility, because our education and experience enable us to command so many facts to support our position. At that time, we're part of the problem, not the solution.

How to Reverse Our Barriers and Parlay Them Into New Ideas

Writing down everything we know, or believe to be true, about a problem or situation is the difference between using our background to generate new ideas, or letting our background limit our mental flexibility.

To avoid letting our experience and education do our thinking for us, we have decided to write down everything we know about the problem or situation at hand. After we write it down, we can look at every piece of information that has a bearing on the current situation, and determine whether or not that information is applicable and, if so, under what circumstances. If our information isn't applicable, we can put it aside, or replace it with more meaningful information.

To help us get an additional handle on this concept, we'll take a problem and identify the barriers for it, and then use those restraints to initiate new ideas.

The School System Problem

Assume you are a member of our local school board. As is the case in much of the United States, the number of students in your school system has been declining over the past ten years. You recognize that eventually the school system will have to look at a more economical method of delivering quality education to the local children.

In anticipation of this future cutback, you decide to do some creative thinking on how education could be delivered at less cost. You have been a member of the board for a number of years, so you already have a lot of information in your head that is important. You know, for instance, that some curriculum can't be discontinued due to state law. You know also that all of the school buildings vary in their cost of operation, and what those costs are. Finally, you know that this problem has been discussed at board meetings before, and nothing of consequence has come out of it.

Rather than permitting your background in this matter to be a barrier to your thinking, you decide to list everything that you know, or believe to be true, about the situation. This information fund includes the following:

- The current system delivers quality education.
- The existence of school buildings limits flexibility.
- Citizens see the problem, but don't want to make sacrifices to arrive at solutions.
- Current teachers are very capable.
- Current teachers do a good job educating the children.
- If we have fewer pupils, we will need fewer teachers.
- If we have fewer pupils, we receive fewer dollars from the state.
- Many school programs are mandated by the state.
- Utility costs in the buildings are comparatively inflexible.
- Teacher costs are directly related to the number of teachers on staff.
- School buildings are required.
- Federal guidelines on asbestos must be met.
- New equipment is constantly required to maintain an up-to-date education, i.e. computers.
- Busing creates artificial expense.
- School operates for nine months out of the year.
- There likely isn't just one solution to this problem.
- The policy of tenure distorts recognition of quality teachers.
- Students often do not respect the school's property.
- Students need twelve nine month years to graduate.
- The length of time needed to graduate is historically fixed.
- There is no competition for providing an education to our children.

Having created this list of information, you know that one of the dangers of the above is that these ideas, if not frequently challenged, will limit your creativity. As a matter of fact, the more of these ideas you have, the less likely you will be to permit new ideas to grow in your mind.

By writing them down, you place yourself in the enviable position of having a lot of experience in this issue (i.e., reflected in the large number of diverse ideas you're able to write down), and having the flexibility to see these ideas as possible growth points.

There is another reason to put this list together. Not only is it of value to challenge each of these beliefs, they also provide the core of every creative idea you will have.

One of the ways to encourage this use of your existing ideas is by critically reviewing the list of restraints that you generated above. If you assess each of them, it not only provides an opportunity to evaluate their applicability in this situation, but may also trigger new ideas. To test this, let's take a look at some of the information on the list you created for your school board problem.

- The current system delivers quality education.

(True enough, but that doesn't preclude the existence of other systems that could produce an education as good, or perhaps better.)

- The existence of school buildings limits flexibility.

(Equally true. We needn't feel we're married to these buildings, though—they do have a value in the marketplace. If we chose to sell them, it would provide cash, and a reduction in utilities and overhead expenses. NOTE: would it be possible to rent currently existing facilities that are under-utilized?)

- Citizens see the problem, but don't want to make sacrifices to find a solution.

(Citizen flexibility is often related to the options available for solving a problem. That is, if parents see that sacrifices must be made to keep the school system functional, they will make those sacrifices rather than shut the whole system down. Creating support for a new idea, then, may be a result of carefully timed unattractive options.)

- Current teachers are very capable.

(True. Not only are they capable, we owe them some sense of job security. That doesn't mean, however, that we are locked into our current format and facilities.)

- If we have fewer pupils, we'll need fewer teachers.

(Obviously true, but an extremely difficult relationship for teachers and parents to grasp. Does the relationship of teachers to students have to remain at the current level? Can we somehow reduce the number of teachers more quickly than the reduction in number of students?)

- If we have fewer pupils, we'll receive fewer dollars from the state.

(This isn't just number of pupils in the district, it is actually the number of pupils who attend the requisite number of school days. Maybe we need to work on improving attendance.)

- Many school programs are mandated by the state.

(The programs are mandated, but is the manner in which the program is administered also mandated? How much flexibility do we have in the execution of the program?)

- Utility costs in the buildings are comparatively inflexible.

(Perhaps the most flexible part of this is the number of buildings involved, rather than the cost of utilities in each building.)

- Teacher costs are directly related to the number of teachers on staff.

(Not completely true. The cost of teachers is also dependent upon the seniority of the teaching staff, and the number of full-time versus part-time teachers.)

Each of the ideas you list demonstrates your experience and knowledge in the area of schools and school finances. Making decisions solely on this information would assure us the ability to manage status quo in any school system. However, the current situation dictates that change is required.

Left unchallenged, no matter what the problem might be in your school system, this information would likely lead you to a decision of no change.

Since conditions suggest that change is essential, you have to reevaluate your knowledge to see if new ideas are more appropriate.

After reviewing the above information, you might come up with some of the following options.

- Consolidate schools.
- Consolidate churches and schools, so buildings will be utilized seven days per week.
- Initiate larger class sizes, reducing the need for as many teachers.
- Conduct school twelve months per year.
- Cut all salaries.
- Cut out all outside activities.
- Make the principal's job include teaching in smaller schools.

The first reason for writing your ideas down was to see if all of these preconceived notions (or barriers) were still valid. Those that were not, we removed from our store of ready information or modified them to fit. Those that were, we left for further consideration.

Your second reason for writing down these preconceived notions (barriers) was to see if in so doing we could jar loose some creative ideas. We were at least partially successful, as shown in the list of ideas above. While none of them are startling, they are a good start toward finding unique and constructive options.

The Chicago Traffic Problem

Most of us are aware of the rush hour traffic gridlock in most major cities. This will be the foundation for our next creative challenge.

Assume you are an assistant to the mayor of the city of Chicago. His Honor has noticed that the traffic in his delightful city has become heavy. As a matter of fact, it has become intolerable! One afternoon, as you and the boss are traveling between meetings, the boss glares back at you and says, "I'm sick of having my life flash before my eyes every time we go down an expressway ramp. I'm tired of waiting in traffic jams that are so huge they affect Milwaukee. Half of the friends I have I met in the car next to me during one of these vehicular work stoppages. I'm sick of the traffic. Fix it!"

Since rationality is one of the criteria for being an assistant to the mayor, you point out that the traffic "is what it is." The mayor seems unmoved by the logic of your response, and encourages you to have your recommendations ready for the next meeting, some two weeks hence. Your contribution to this issue seems inevitable. So you start!

Fortunately, you have just read an extremely beneficial book on the subject of creativity. This book indicates that many of the barriers to your creativity are a result of your knowledge and experience. To be sure that this vague generalization doesn't apply to you, you decide to make a list of everything you know, or believe to be true, about the traffic problem in Chicago. By doing so, you will be able to evaluate every piece of information and validate its appropriateness in light of the present situation.

The following are a few of the things you know, or believe to be true, about the traffic problem in Chicago.

- The problem is with surface transportation.
- People won't take public transportation.
- Most cars tend to be on the road at the same time.
- People won't car-pool.
- There isn't enough money available to fix the problem.
- People don't work where they live.
- There is no single fix. It likely will require more than one cure.
- Any cure will likely not have the cooperation of other contiguous political bodies (this is a well-known fact of life in Chicago politics).

Well, the book was wrong! This is not a list of barriers! A more solid collection of truths would be hard to come by. Having finished this initial list, you leave it on your desk, ready to move on to more meaningful endeavors. A junior staff member absently picks up the list and looks it over. In response to his question about its contents, you indicate that this is a "list of undeniable truths concerning the traffic problem in Chicago." Each, you continue, is another reason why nothing of consequence can be done about it.

After maintaining a few minutes of respectful silence, your junior associate offers a few observations.

- Surely we have options other than surface transportation. Chicago has a substantial above and below ground system already in place.
- It's true that most people, if given a choice, don't want to take public transportation. Taxes can be used to encourage it, though. Not only that, mightn't there be a way to take advantage of the dislike of taxes by combining public and private transportation?

- Yes, most cars are on the road at the same time. But many cities have had success with encouraging staggered starts with firms in the downtown area.
- Most people don't want to car-pool, but that doesn't mean that they can't be shown the benefits of doing so; or the penalties of not doing so.

Your junior staff member is taking the same ideas that you see as restraints, and making them the foundation of innovative thinking! In your defense, you decide to do the same thing with the remaining barriers. What do you come up with?

Each of the above ideas which you identified as barriers to your flexibility in solving the problem of traffic in Chicago, was actually a source of innovation when seen differently. If you hadn't written these barriers down, you would have continued to let them dominate your thinking. After you wrote them down and analyzed them, you could see that they were not the limiting factor that you initially assumed.

By reviewing Chapter Two and the different types of barriers we face in our creative efforts, we can find other ideas that serve as restraints. Some of the *boundaries* that limit our thinking include:

- # of miles of roads
- # of drivers
- # of Chicago residents
- # of people who work in Chicago and live elsewhere
- # of working hours in a day or week
- # of traffic complaints
- # of policemen
- # of lanes of traffic
- # of dollars available to fix the problem

If we add barriers that are *limited options*, we would include:

- Either we are dealing with public transportation or

private transportation.

- The solution has to be financed with public or private money.

What additional facts can you come up with relative to the problem of traffic in Chicago that fall into the categories of:

Guiding Principle:
Historical Factors:
Assumptions:

How to Turn Quantity Into Quality in Your Ideas

There is an old saying that indicates, "If you want good ideas, get lots of ideas."

If we look around for that single pearl of an idea, rejecting lesser suggestions along the way, we're not likely to come up with any breakthrough innovations. As a matter of fact, some of our more notably "creative people" have prospered not by single successes, but through repeated failures! Thomas Edison failed thousands of times before he perfected the light bulb. In this case Mr. Edison was, in fact, not a particularly creative person, just persistent.

Typically, we will generate our truly innovative ideas after reviewing many others that had little promise. While this may initially seem like a waste of time, it is not. For every poor idea, we will find that the review of that idea forced us to look at our situation from a slightly different direction. Every time we do that, we are inviting other suggestions into consideration.

If we're willing to concede that the more ideas we generate, the more likely we will be to come up with the best idea, then doesn't it make sense to improve our ability to come up with a large number of ideas? This next section shows us how to do that. Not only will it help us come up with many ideas, it will show us how to improve our ability to do so.

To help us use this technique, and measure our progress, we need a scale on which we can gauge our progress. We'll use the following numeric scale to evaluate our ability to come up with a large number of ideas.

Fluency - 1 Point

If our objective is to generate a quantity of ideas, then the first measure should be the absolute number of ideas we're able to develop. We aren't at all concerned about the quality of these ideas. As we have already seen, even bad ideas can lead to good ones. So for now our list will include bad ideas. We don't care if they are reasonable, "do-able," or antisocial. Just as long as they provide a solution to solve whatever problem we're working on at the time. Each of these ideas is worth one point.

Flexibility - 5 Points

Flexibility is defined as the ability to see an issue from several different perspectives. If we were asked to name a new street, and the only options we could come up with were names of former Presidents of the United States, then we wouldn't be very flexible. If, however, our suggested names came from former presidents, types of trees, and signs of the Zodiac, then we'd be considered much more flexible. As a matter of fact, this ability of thinking flexibly is so important we have given it a point value of five for each category of use.

As an example, assume we have been asked to come up with as many uses as we can for steel ball bearings. No matter how much we concentrate on the problem, the only use we can see for ball bearings is to reduce friction. As a result, our suggestions include: using in roller skates, in wheel bearings, and record player turntables.

Based on our scoring above, we would receive only five points for flexibility, as all our suggestions dealt with one type of application, the reduction of friction. If we had been able to think of a single application that dealt with using ball bearings for another type of use, we would have received ten points, five each for two entirely different types of applications.

The ability to be *flexible* in our thinking is the key not only to creativity, but also to progressive improvement in this exercise.

Originality - 10 Points

Depending upon how our mind works, this measure can be a gold mine. Each time we list an idea that is, for us, truly unique, we give ourselves ten points for that idea. Suppose you were asked to list as many uses as possible for a brick. As you develop your list, it suddenly occurs to you that a brick could be used to discipline the neighbor's cat. You write this down, and note to yourself that this is a genuinely unique idea for you. Maybe for someone else this idea would come as a natural, but not for you. Give yourself ten points for each idea that strikes you as personally innovative. As we are self-scoring, we obviously will have to use some restraint in our self-flattery.

The key of this exercise is not the total points scored, but the improvement in total points each time we do the exercise. To assure your true progress, it is important to score yourself as consistently as possible. If you choose to be liberal with your score, be liberal each time you use this tool.

Since the objective of every game is to do well, let's see how we could improve our scores. First, we'll try a simple example. In the next five minutes make a complete list of uses for empty plastic milk cartons. Write each idea down, and work as rapidly s you can.

Assume that after five minutes your list looks like the following:

1. Fishing float
2. Swimming pool marker
3. Sand scoop
4. Milk container
5. Container for recycled oil
6. Container for hazardous wastes
7. Table lamp
8. Garden scarecrow
9. Pouring funnel
10. Candle base
11. Decorative faces

To determine our score we first give ourselves one point for every idea we listed. This gives our initial score as 11, since we have eleven ideas. This is our *fluency* score.

Now in addition to these eleven points, we're also going to give ourselves five points for every category of idea, which will reflect our *flexibility*. Returning to our eleven ideas, we find that ideas 1 and 2 both deal with floating. None of the other ideas do. We give ourselves five points for this category.

Items 3 and 9 both pertain to using the milk cartons to transfer material from one place to another. Another five points for this type of application. Items 4, 5 and 6 all take advantage of the ability of a milk carton to carry liquids. Five points for this type of use. Items 7 and 10 both utilize the milk carton as a decorative accessory; five more points for this category of use.

Items 8 and 11 are each uniquely different, so each is worth five points.

Our score after the first two categories of measure is: 11 for *fluency* (the ability to name a large number of uses), and 30 points for *flexibility* (the ability to see different categories of uses) since there are six categories of use.

As you can see, the ability to be flexible is much more important than the ability to be fluent. This becomes even more apparent with our last scoring opportunity.

Going through our list of eleven uses for the last time, we now see if we've been able to generate any really unusual suggestions. These will give us our *originality* score. Since this is a judgment call, it is very difficult to score yourself. It is also impossible for anyone else to score you. Remember that the criterion for a 10 point originality score is if the idea is unique for you, not someone else.

Perhaps an example will help you see how this works. I was conducting a seminar in Louisiana for a group of executives several years ago. When we came to the point in the workshop where I asked them to score their mental flexibility, they were required to list as many uses as they could for a brick. After the allotted time, I wrote their uses on the blackboard as they were dictated to me.

I was about half-way through when one of them suggested using bricks for jewelry. The group came to a complete stop! The image of bricks hanging from ears and around necks brought our session to a howling standstill. Still laughing, I indicated that we certainly would give that suggestion ten points for *originality*. The volunteer who supplied us with this unique example said that in all honesty, this would not be worth ten points to him. He explained that his hobby was homemade jewelry. At home he had a small tumbler he used to polish rocks that would be placed in a jewelry setting. Since he began with this hobby, he couldn't look at anything that was at all like a stone without visualizing it in a jewelry setting. Therefore, he naturally thought of his hobby when he saw the uses for bricks.

For us, this suggestion would surely be worth ten points as an original idea. For my executive friend in

Louisiana, that wasn't the case, and he was honest enough to say so.

Going back to our original example, I believe that using milk cartons for garden scarecrows would be an original suggestion if offered from me and, therefore, worth ten points.

Our total score in this example is 11 for fluency, 30 for flexibility, and 10 for originality, or 51 in all. This is a good total for our first attempt to think more flexibly. It was mentioned previously that the key to generating high scores in this game is the ability to become more flexible. You might reasonably contest that, since it is the original ideas that bring most of the points.

To be classified as original, an idea has to be unique to you! So where do you find those original ideas? The best method for generating original ideas is to expand your thinking into areas you normally wouldn't pursue; which is *flexibility*. For instance, assume you're looking for a list of ideas to encourage employee participation in a retirement plan. As you create the list, you decide to add financial incentives, a new category of idea. This new category triggers several other suggestions, including buying back the employee's paycheck at a premium. The premium could be the employer's share of the retirement plan. The obvious benefit of this is the promotional advantage. The employee can easily understand how he will gain from participation.

You feel that this idea is worth ten points for originality. The seed for this idea was the mental exploration into a new category of idea, or *flexibility*. This is how most truly original suggestions are born. Learn to expand the number of categories of ideas (flexibility). This will lead to originality.

In sum, if you and I wish to generate creative ideas, we need to be able to generate a lot of ideas. The technique described here will help you develop that discipline. Not only does it give you a means of measuring your progress, it also shows how to continually improve your results.

Mind Expansion Exercises

1. Give yourself three minutes to list as many uses as you can for one of the items listed below. Score yourself with the instrument presented in this chapter.

safety pins
concrete clocks
empty plastic milk cartons
yesterday's newspaper
used automobile tires
paper clips
ball bearings
ballpoint pens
used automobile pistons
used clothing
light bulbs
used batteries
pencil leads
tin cans
junk cars
zippers
fish aquarium
coal
thumbtacks
old mattresses
styrofoam cups
pop bottles
sand
sawdust
horse hair
baby shoes
straight pins

2. Now refer to one of the problems you listed in the first chapter, and give yourself five minutes to note every conceivable solution to that problem, whether the solution is rational or not. Score yourself as above.

3. You have just been told that your department budget is due in three weeks. You also have been advised to sharpen your pencil, as top management wants an overall cut in expenses of 10%. You know that you actually need an additional 20% to run your department most efficiently. List everything you know, or believe to be true, about this problem. Then challenge each of those "facts" in light of your current situation.

For potential approaches to the above problems, refer to the "Possibilities" section at the end of this book.

Chapter Four:

Developing Your "Off-Road" Thinking Skills

SUMMARY OF CHAPTER THREE:

1. Due to its importance in personal creativity, we concentrated on developing our ability to use our creativity barriers to spur additional innovative ideas. Two examples, a financially strapped school district and heavy traffic in a major metropolitan area, were used. These examples demonstrated how our experience and education can be used to create new ideas.
2. To help us gauge our progress, we introduced a method of measuring our creative output, and discussed how to use this tool to increase the flexibility of our thinking. By applying this technique, we can learn to force ourselves into more innovative thinking.
3. The key to coming up with more innovative ideas is our increase in flexibility. This is the origin of all creative ideas.

CHAPTER FOUR OBJECTIVES:

1. Five principles guide our progress in the development of innovative ideas. Understanding each of these principles will enable us to stretch our mental flexibility.
2. Another product of our education and experience

is our basic philosophical approach to thinking. The approach we have used throughout our career is appropriate for much of our mental activity, but not for creative thinking. Another approach will be discussed here. An approach that utilizes less discipline, and is more inclined to help us generate innovative ideas.

3. "Triggers," or insights, that lead to spontaneous thinking will be introduced, and their value discussed.

The Principles of Creative Thinking

As in most disciplines, creative thinking also revolves around certain basic concepts. These concepts enable us to better understand how creativity works, and how it can be nurtured.

While the process of thinking creatively is actually one of reduced mental discipline, there are actually certain principles we should understand from the beginning. If we lodge these principles firmly in our mind while proceeding through this book, it will enhance our understanding. As you will see, no one of them is difficult; they just require a different mind-set.

Principle Number One

The only truly bad ideas are those that die without giving rise to other ideas.

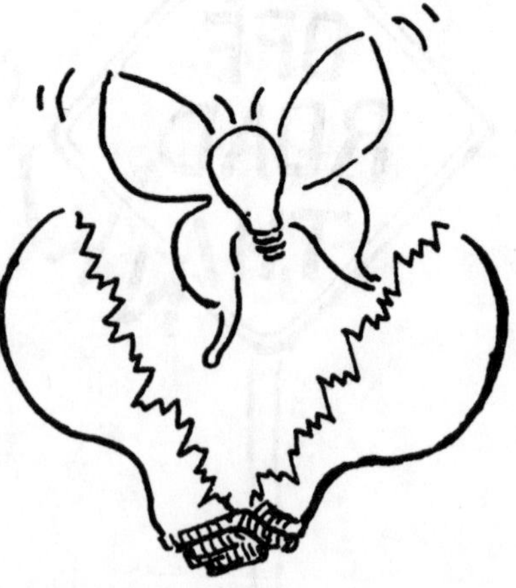

While patently simple in its phrasing, this principle is difficult to execute. It means that no idea is ever considered to be fodder for criticism. You probably recognize this as a modification of your basic "brainstorming" training, where all ideas are to be treated positively. The purpose here is somewhat different, as we are suggesting that we not only refrain from criticizing an idea, we are also responsible for using each idea as a basis for other, more applicable alternatives.

Principle Number Two

If you want good ideas, you need a lot of ideas.

All of us suffer from the urge to come up with a single idea that will change the direction of the earth's rotation. This urge is perfectly understandable; we all see ourselves as capable of such breakthrough insights. This will be a mistake for most of us, since each true breakthrough is normally preceded by other, more modest contributions. Resist the temptation to reject lesser suggestions. Understand that they are all the foundation for breakthrough ideas to come. In addition, one of the measures of creative ability is pure volume of ideas. We don't want to sacrifice that.

Principle Number Three

Few of our ideas will be viewed as a 'breakthrough,' but when they are added together, the sum of all of them could well be a 'breakthrough.'

When we begin practicing the techniques advanced in this book, there is a natural tendency to be somewhat disappointed by the quality of our suggestions. They just don't seem to provide the unique insights we had hoped for. Remember that every unique idea is based on other ideas that precede it. If we don't have a history of creative thoughts, we have nothing from which to build.

Principle Number Four

It doesn't matter if it 'ain't broke,' it can probably use fixing anyway.

One of the serious detriments to our innovative

thought processes is that we look for things to "fix." In most cases there is little conspicuously wrong with the way things are done now. As a result, we spend little time offering suggestions that will result in continual improvement. It is this notion of continual improvement that gives us the greatest opportunity for new ideas.

Principle Number Five

Great ideas are nothing more than the reordering of things we already know.

The notion that great ideas simply fall out of the skies gives creativity much too mystic an air. The simple truth of the matter is this: we can't come up with ideas that apply information we do not currently have! If these ideas are based on information we have, how can we trigger insights with old data? All of creative thinking is the mixing and blending of information currently held in our mind. The skill isn't one of generating new information, it is one of reordering the information at our disposal. The ability to mix and blend information is the keystone of this book.

The natural conclusion of this principle might be stretched to read, "I don't need to learn anything new." This is an unattractive conclusion and certainly not one that we support. While your current knowledge base provides the food for all of your creative ideas, this does not imply that we should stop learning. After all, based on this definition, every additional piece of information we learn increases our number of potential creative ideas as a multiple of everything we have previously known!

The Value of "Off-Road" Thinking

Our education and experience to date has been based on the idea that there is a benefit in thinking like others have thought before us. As a result, we are taught the information generated by great thinkers in hopes of emulating them. One mental skill which has not been developed is our ability to use illogical thought processes.

There are two ways in which we can mentally approach any problem or situation. The first is best shown by our academic training, where we are taught what to do based on what has been done. We refer to this type of thinking as "commuter traffic" thinking.

This is "commuter traffic" thinking because it is analogous to driving in commuter traffic in the morning. All cars are headed in the same direction, at basically the same speed. The pattern of the traffic is set by the group, and the individual is lost in the movement of the majority. Any individual involved in commuter traffic must abide by the flow of the group. If the individual deviates from the pattern of the group, she will crash.

We use this thinking to fit with the group; to duplicate ideas and suggestions that have been made in the past. With this approach, we verify our expertise by saying that which is expected, and doing that which is predictable.

The second type of mental approach is "off-road" thinking. Where "commuter traffic" thinking follows the thought process set by others, "off-road" thinking establishes its own parameters. "Off-road" thinking is willing to deviate from the norm.

Following our analogy, the off-road driving experience is very different than that of the commuter traffic driving experience. In off-road driving there are few roads, many uncharted paths, and an infinite number of previously untraveled directions. If you choose to turn right, you do so. You can go left, stop, back up, or just sit where you choose. Your chosen direction is a product of personal inspiration and urge, and not that of the other traffic around you.

For the sake of brevity and clarity as well, we'll refer to "off-road" thinking in this text as OR thinking. Not only do these initials represent an abbreviation of "off-road," they also indicate the true purpose of this thought process, that of creating options. Thus the word "or." Similarly, we will refer to "commuter traffic" thinking in this text as CT.

To give you a practical example of this approach, review the problem below.

In the NCAA basketball championships, 64 teams from all over the United States are invited to compete. The championship is single elimination, as teams are eliminated after a single loss. What is the minimum number of matches that must be played to find the national champion?

In working with groups across the country I have received answers ranging from 1 to 64. The correct answer is 63. If you got the correct answer, congratulations. I am, however, more interested in the method you used to arrive at your answer than I am with the answer itself.

If you approached this problem like most of us do, you likely began by figuring 32 initial games. The winners of these games, all 32 of them, would meet in another 16 games. These winners would then meet in 8 contests, etc. The total, if you add up the eventual sequence above, is 63 games.

This approach of following the winners is an example of commuter traffic (CT) thinking. If you were an off-road (OR) thinker, you might be willing to approach the problem from a totally different direction. Notice that the CT thinker started with the winners at each level and added each successful group of contestants together to arrive at the correct number. The OR thinker might decide that he or she could get to the same conclusion more quickly by following the losers rather than the winners.

If you have 64 entrants in a single elimination tournament, how many times can each participant lose before they are eliminated?

Once, right?

Of the sixty-four teams, how many will lose?

Sixty-three, right?

How many times will they lose?

Once, right?

Therefore, there have to be enough matches for everyone to lose once except the winner, or 63 total matches.

This is an example of how an OR thinker might view a problem, and the path to solution of that problem, differently than most of us. The OR thinkers give themselves permission to begin with the losers rather than the winners. His or her solution was as correct as that of the CT thinker, it just took less time to get there.

Our point here is not that we should follow the losers to become OR thinkers, but that we should be willing to think differently from the norm to perceive new, potentially beneficial solutions.

Just as we see the OR thinker looking at things from a different perspective (in this case from the standpoint of the losers), we need to change our mental directions to spur more innovative ideas. If you recall from an earlier section of this book, I told the story of a friend who had offered a solution to the problem of high employee turnover, which was to tie their legs together.

This approach is a clear example of OR thinking. If we were in that board room, I wonder what types of suggestions we would make to solve the problem of turnover? Some of them might include:

- Incentive system
- Better work conditions

- Subtle coercion
- More money
- Better management
- Day care facilities
- Contracts
- More participation

In any "right thinking" board room, these options would surely come up. They are all CT thoughts, rather than OR thoughts. We refer to them as commuter traffic because they represent the results of our many years of handling problems just like this one. These suggestions are a product of our education and experience. All of them are logical, well documented answers to the problem. All are presented with the sincere intention of giving a solution. Most importantly, they are all "correct," and we have learned that we must always provide "correct" answers.

Breaking the "Correct Connection"

The ultimately correct solution to a problem does not have to come from a correct suggestion.

We share a basic belief about our decision making processes. We don't hold this belief because we read it anywhere, since it hasn't been written. No teacher passed it on to us in the confidence of an after hours consultation. We won't pass it on to our kids, because it is so obvious to do so would be an insult. Unfortunately, despite our conviction as to the accuracy of this belief, it is entirely false!

That belief is this: we believe that every ultimately "correct" solution comes from equally "correct" suggestions. In the context of the high employee turnover problem, wouldn't you expect that the ultimately correct solution to that problem would come from modifications of the options we listed above? Let's take a look at how that conversation might go.

First the suggestion is made that an incentive system be initiated. That sounds good, but it could be too expensive. So we look for something to reinforce or enhance that suggestion. Better work conditions sounds good, and as a capital investment, it's easier to spread the cost over time. Adding coercion, money and management in proper doses certainly couldn't hurt. After a period of time, we believe the ultimately "correct" solution will come from a combination of these equally "correct" options.

We believe that this process of culling "correct" ideas to find the ultimately correct solution is not only attractive, but necessary. Based on our story, however, we know that this isn't the case. The best solution came from an improper suggestion that was clearly "incorrect." Despite the fact that we feel the best solution will be found at the top of a stack of other reasonable ideas, nothing could be further from the truth.

If we blindly let our experience and education lead us along the path of CT thinking, we'll never be able to generate the truly innovative solutions that we want. This capacity to think beyond our education and experience is the capacity for OR thinking.

OR thinking is the ability to see the suggestion to "tie employees' legs together" as a step toward other, more applicable suggestions. Let's face it; if we were dumb enough to make that suggestion at most board meetings, the only product might well be our availability in the job market. An OR thinking board saw the idea as a starting point and worked from there. A CT board would have killed the idea, and not used it to generate other suggestions.

To understand the differences between off-road (OR) and commuter traffic (CT) thinking, review the columns on the following page. In the left hand column, characteristics are shown for a CT thinker. The contrasting characteristics are shown in the right hand column for the OR thinker.

COMMUTER TRAFFIC (CT) THINKER	OFF-ROAD (OR) THINKER
1. Deals with absolutes	1. Deals with opportunities
2. Believes the only avenue to correct answers is through correct suggestions	2. Recognizes the value of frivolous thinking
3. Looks for optimum solutions	3. Seeks alternative ways
4. Stops thinking at "no"	4. Uses "no" as a bridge to other ideas
5. Works well with facts	5. Works well with concepts
6. Concentrates on discipline	6. Sets discipline aside at appropriate time
7. Invites logical paths	7. Welcomes any path

Our ability to use CT thinking has been superbly developed by our education, as well as by our professional and life experiences. In many cases, however, the path to innovation is not through this highly disciplined form of thinking, but through the freer form offered by off-road (OR) thinking.

With so little experience in using it, the trick is being able to trigger OR thinking when we want it. One of the best ways to do this is to consciously remove from our thought processes the rules, laws, and dictates that subtly guide our current thinking.

Assume for the moment that we can remove from our moral makeup any sense of social conscience, moral limits, or concern for our fellow man. If we could do that and look again at our problem of employee turnover, what solutions might come to mind? We could lock the doors, kidnap their children to force compliance, chain them to their work stations, lend them so much money that we could force servitude, or fire them before they can quit.

None of these ideas can stand the test of logic or reasonableness. Each of them abandons one or more precepts that we hold dear. As an OR thinker, however, this is unimportant. We know that the value of the suggestion lies not in the suggestion itself, but in the new ground that the suggestion breaks.

For instance, the idea of kidnapping children to reduce turnover is offensive. When we look at that idea, it could bring to mind that good quality day care facilities are difficult to obtain. Perhaps if we started a day care facility for the children of our employees, this benefit could be perceived as attractive enough to reduce turnover. We have effectively "kidnapped their children" to reduce turnover.

Firing employees before they quit hardly seems like an intelligent alternative. We could, however, make the career development of our employees such a key objective that their constant path upward would be part of their job description. In effect, we're "firing" them at one level to qualify them for the next level.

Where Commuter Traffic (CT) Thinking Fits

Before any suggestion can be applied, it must first stand the test of CT (commuter traffic) thinking. While OR (off-road) provides the best environment for innovation, CT thinking is necessary to clearly identify the applicability of ideas.

The above example is not meant to demean the value of CT thinking. As you have read along, it is apparent that any idea we suggest to solve a problem must stand the test of CT thinking. Both of these methods of thinking deserves a place in your thinking arsenal. When it is time to consider new and inventive ideas, we should be wearing our OR thinking cap. When it is time to evaluate the ideas that are a product of our OR thinking, it is time for our CT thinking skills.

To provide a perspective into the relative value of CT

thinking, review the situation below, and offer suggestions in the space provided.

For the last six months, you have been increasingly frustrated in your job. Despite the fact that a number of your suggestions to top management have been adopted, you have received no direct recognition. Not only that, but two promotions have been offered to your less productive co-workers.

You decide to discuss it with your boss, and as you pass his secretary to enter his office you notice that your latest memo containing another suggestion for improvement is on the screen of her word processor. While it is the same memo you submitted, your name has been replaced by his. What do you do?

____

____

You have likely listed two types of suggestions above. The first respects the rules as established, and attempts to operate within those rules. The second disregards those rules and tends to be more innovative. Even if the more innovative suggestions break some rules, we aren't bothered by that. After all, their only purpose was to spur our creative juices in the first place.

Some of the suggestions which break the rules could include:

- Meet him in the parking lot, get him by the throat, and measure how far out his jugular vein will bulge.
- Suggest that you know where his children go to school, and list the hazards the poor tykes might face along that route.
- Offer several activities in which your boss might engage, each of which would cause him to walk funny.

These are all OR suggestions, and are likely not to survive the burden of logic. Their purpose is not to be logical, or even rational. Rather, they are to provide a basis for other, more socially acceptable, alternatives.

The key to OR thinking is the ability to think outside the rules. Set aside every barrier that limits idea generation. Included in this barriers are our education and experience, our moral and ethical structure, as well as other self imposed limits. Certainly we won't make our final decision without these restraints, but we're not going to let them stop us from thinking flexibly at the start of the process.

Exposing Yourself to Mental "Triggers"

A "trigger" is a vehicle which provides the bridge between two pieces of dissimilar information. This bridge creates innovative ideas, and should be deliberately developed.

Earlier, we discussed the concept that creative ideas came to us via a "thunderbolt." Aside from the mystic appeal of this idea, we now know that this analogy isn't particularly accurate. Ideas do come to us quickly, but normally as a result of the marriage of two or more previously dissimilar pieces of information.

The real "thunderbolt," then, is the path, or "trigger" that connects these pieces of information. We can create these paths, or "triggers," by forcing ourselves to perceive things differently than we normally would, or by forcing relationships between unrelated data.

This skill is important to our innovative growth, and will constitute a major portion of the remainder of this book.

Mind Expansion Exercises

1. One of your salespeople is constantly ignoring current customers. This salesperson is gifted, but tends to see the sale as consummated when the order is taken, and doesn't see the importance of maintaining contact with the customer. List as many solutions to this problem as you can; then identify your solutions as "off-road" (these suggestions will tend to ignore the rules), or "commuter traffic" in their orientation. "Commuter traffic" suggestions will tend to follow a "correct" line of thought.

2. Now do this same exercise for one of the problems you identified in the second chapter. Try to apply this technique to a problem you haven't addressed earlier in this book.

For potential approaches to the above problems, refer to the "Possibilities" section at the end of this book.

Chapter Five:
Increasing Our Mental Elasticity

SUMMARY OF CHAPTER FOUR:

1. Five basic principles guide our innovative thinking. Understanding them is a requisite for our continued growth. They are:
   a. The only bad ideas are those that die without giving rise to other ideas.
   b. If you want good ideas, you need a lot of ideas.
   c. Few of our ideas will be viewed as a "breakthrough," but when they are added together, the sum of all of them could well be a "breakthrough."
   d. It doesn't matter if it "ain't broke," it can probably use fixing anyway.
   e. Great ideas are nothing more than the reordering of things we already know.
2. There are two opposing approaches for our thinking. The first is "commuter traffic" (CT) thinking, which is represented by the disciplined thinking we are taught to use in school. The second is "off-road" (OR) thinking, which has less regard for history, principles and rules. CT thinking is essential for identifying the applicability of alternative suggestions. OR thinking is essential for developing uniquely beneficial ideas.

3. Mental "triggers" are the paths followed by the connection of dissimilar information in our minds, which results in unique insights, or creative ideas.

OBJECTIVES OF CHAPTER FIVE:

1. In our thinking, we unconsciously recognize allegiance to a myriad of laws. This allegiance, if set aside temporarily, can help us generate new ideas.
2. Creating fantasy situations will help us generate innovative ideas. Two techniques for imposing fantasy on ourselves will be introduced in this chapter.

We have already discussed the concept that if we want good ideas, we need to generate many ideas. Not only have we talked about this, we have also developed a technique for measuring our output of ideas. Our previous exposure to this technique suggested we find multiple uses for commonly known items.

Now we'll use that same technique to come up with ideas that are a bit more practical.

Assume for the moment that you have a job as a street sweeper. When you first accepted the job, you felt that it might lead into something more beneficial for you. As time has gone by, you find that movement out of the job, if any, will have to be initiated by you. In the interim, you decide to take best advantage of this seemingly menial task yourself. List below the ways you could profit from your experience as a street sweeper, and score yourself using the scale described in Chapter Three.

____

____

____

You may find your score has dropped below what you have come to expect from yourself. There is a very simple explanation for this phenomenon. Your ability to generate high scores with this technique is inversely proportional to your familiarity with the problem. The closer you are to the problem, the less likely you are to see a solution.

While you may not be a street sweeper, the notion of parlaying an existing job into a more significant work experience is common to all of us. Contrast this to the problem of finding many uses for a plastic milk carton. You are not only not close to that problem, you could really care less. This is what gives you the capacity to think flexibly about uses for milk cartons; it isn't a problem for you.

During our conversations on OR and CT thinking, we make an assumption that we are all able to use OR thinking. In working with groups across the country, I have found that this is not always the case. In some instances, our sense of discipline is so strong that we simply can't think in a different way. While this is difficult to overcome, there is a method we have developed to help in that process.

Operating Outside the Law

Through training and life experiences, we learn to accept certain limits to our flexibility. One of the most notable and impactful of these limits is our adherence to multiple sets of laws. Since these laws have governed us throughout our lives, and generally operate below the level of consciousness, they represent a serious block to our mental flexibility.

Throughout our lives, we have been taught, and properly, that a citizen must behave in certain predictable ways. This pattern of behavior is laid out for us through a series of laws. In all of our moves as an independent citizen, we are expected to act in accordance with these laws. Doing so not only assures few unfortunate contacts with legal authorities, but also enables us to mix in society. These laws, then, are essential to our social and legal survival.

In the context of creativity these laws limit the range of our thinking at a time when we don't want our thinking limited; when we wish to use OR thinking. During the time we want to develop OR ideas, we don't want restraints on our mental flexibility, legal or otherwise. The time to consider those restraints is when we have generated our OR suggestions and are ready to move into CT thinking mode.

To assist us in shedding the burden of these laws, consider the types of laws that limit your ability to generate

OR suggestions. Our identification of these laws will help us to think outside the boundaries that they impose.

The first set of laws to which we respond is Roman law. This is the foundation of our legal system, and includes penalties for murder, rape, robbery and other crimes. The impact of these laws is to limit what we are able to do to our fellow man.

The second of these is civil law. These laws deal with the rights of private citizens in this country. While less sensational than Roman law, these laws include traffic regulations and areas of civil disobedience.

While the above two categories of law are well documented and adhered to based on legal precedent and written entries, the remaining laws that we embrace are in many instances not documented, but serve to limit us as seriously.

In this less structured category are moral code, ethical limits, social conscience, and reason.

Moral code, in many instances, is not written down. In much of its application, it is established by considerations of personal responsibility to others. These laws are considered living laws in that they change through application and over time. Moral code would tell us that it is wrong for television evangelists to enrich themselves at the expense of their "flocks." When it was made public that this exact thing was happening, people were shocked and offended, although little had been done that was specifically against Roman law. Similarly, we feel the same way toward our political representatives. These elected representatives should represent our interests at all times, rather than the interests of specific groups.

Ethical limits are established generally through professional conduct. It suggests that professionals, i.e. doctors, lawyers, consultants, not advertise. For a long time it was considered beneath the position of a professional to promote his or her services. Over time that has changed, and we now see their ads on TV, over radio, and in the newspapers.

Another example of ethical limits is the way an employer deals with prospective employees. If a prospective employee applies for a job and is rejected without an interview, it is considered proper, or ethical, to advise them of their rejection through the mail. If, however, the prospective employee is interviewed and then rejected, the rejection should be done either face-to-face or by personal telephone call.

Social conscience is different for everyone and as a result leads to much confusion and disappointment. These laws are not written, but are passed on through common understanding and social contact. Behavior that is governed by these laws includes not talking during the Sunday church sermon, refraining from asking how much weight a person has gained, and not dominating a conversation at a party. Because each of us has a slightly different concept of this series of laws, we frequently find ourselves disappointed with the behavior of others. At the same time, others are often disappointed in us for reasons we don't really understand.

The last type of law to which we respond is that of reason. All the physical sciences have laws which are known to each of us. Some of the most conspicuous examples are the law of gravity and the laws of mathematics. These are frequently considered the least flexible of all laws, as they deal with inviolate principles of physical matter. For this reason they are considered least likely to provide fodder for innovative thought.

To give you an example of how this might not be the case, consider the following problem:

"What is half of 13?"

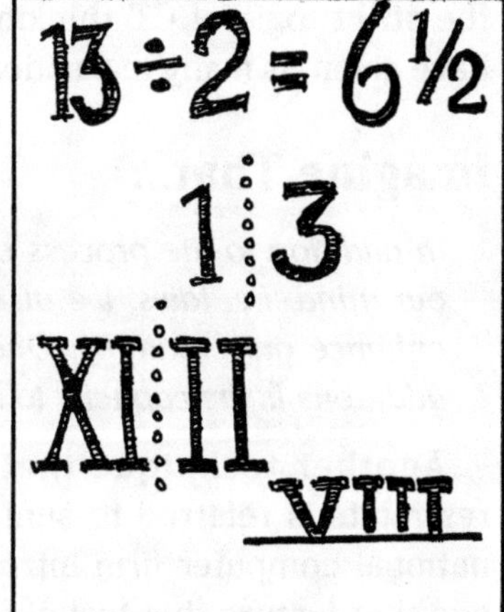

According to your education, this is a one-solution problem; the only correct answer is 6 1/2.

13/2 = 6.5

Using OR thinking we could get severally equally correct answers. If we visualize 13 as two independent digits, which they are, one-half of 13 would be 1 and the other half 3, or:

13 = 1 and 3

If 13 is in Roman numerals, or XIII, the halves become 11 and 2.

XIII = XI and II

Or if our Roman numeral halves are horizontal rather than vertical, the top half becomes 8.

Half of XIII = VIII

We're not likely to impress our third grade teacher with this glowing logic, but it serves to show that there are always optional responses, no matter how restricted our environment is. This is especially meaningful in the above example, as few environments are as restrictive as mathematics.

The purpose of defining laws is to help us see more clearly the kinds of restraints that inhibit our mental flexibility. If in our attempts to use OR thinking, we can generate options that violate these laws, we have created another category of OR ideas. For instance, in our Chicago traffic problem, how many more ideas might we have generated if we had ignored Roman and civil laws? No speed limits, no concerns for the rights of citizens, or the right to enact unfair laws that would solve the problem.

Naturally, none of these OR ideas would have survived the strict logic of CT thinking, but they would certainly have given us many more ideas with which to work.

Imagine That...

In addition to the process of removing some things from our mind, i.e. laws, we also need to add some things to enhance our creativity. One of the most fruitful of these additions is the capacity to fantasize.

Another technique that helps us get around our restraints is referred to simply as "What if..." Recently a national computer firm introduced a series of television ads that feature this technique. Its application is simple, and with some practice, can generate some unique ideas.

Make a statement about your problem or situation that is either stretching the truth or plainly false. In front of that statement you place the words "What if..." Then you attempt to answer the theoretical question you have just asked. Albert Einstein is said to have used this method to advance his understanding of the theory of relativity. According to his biography, Einstein asked himself the question, "What if I was descending in an elevator at the speed of light and there were a hole in the side of the elevator? What would happen if the elevator were to pass through a beam of light?"

What he concluded in his analysis of that scenario is a mystery to most of us, but the use of the "What if..." technique was identified as being invaluable to his exploration. A number of years ago, I used this technique to increase the flexibility of a seminar group with whom I was working in Detroit. We had a relatively small group of about 25 participants, which included three people who worked in automotive styling. I had frankly looked forward to working with this group primarily because of their presence. I had expected to see a real outpouring of innovative ideas from them.

After the first half day, it was clear that I wasn't able to jar their current thinking mode. Worse yet, they had become a negative influence on the rest of the group. During one of the exercises, I walked over to see if there was any way to help them break out of their apparent rigidity. As we talked, I decided that they might respond to an example of "What if..." I asked them to answer the question, "What if...cars were inside out?"

Predictably, the first thing they said was, "but cars aren't inside out!" I assured them I was aware of that, and asked them to answer the question anyway. After a few minutes they reported their ideas to the rest of the group.

If cars were inside out, the upholstery would be on the outside of the vehicle.

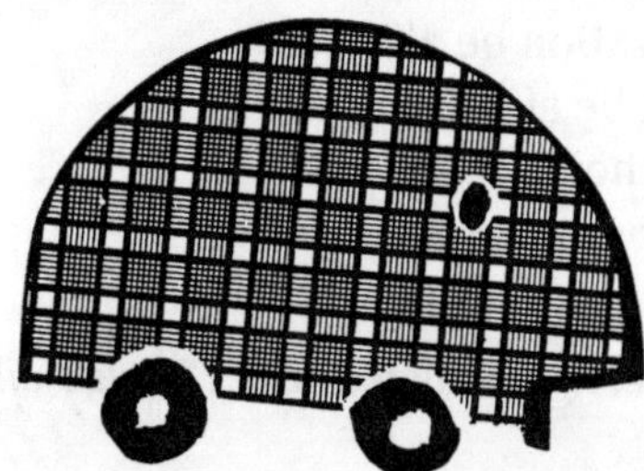

(This wasn't as ridiculous as it sounded, they reported. More progress had recently been made in the durability of cloth than paint. Not only that, applique had already been used on car exteriors for decorative purposes. Since we don't see tweed Oldsmobiles, I have to suspect that this idea didn't go anywhere.)

If cars were inside out, the engine would be fully exposed.

(This was initially dismissed as a profitless idea, until one of the group pointed out that among the "old school" hot-rodders, engines were deliberately exposed for aesthetic appeal. Not only that, motorcycles and snowmobiles still use the well-dressed engine as an aesthetic addition to the vehicle.)

The value of using a stretch of the truth or an untruth in this technique will become more apparent as you apply it. It is easier to expand on our current level of thinking if we are removed from the restraint of reality. One of the ways to do this is to look at the situation from an incorrect or improper position. If we start from an untruth, we begin the exercise with more freedom. After some practice, it will be possible to do the same thing with more solid statements, but for now, this is simpler.

To help you answer your "What if..." question, consider these impacts on the situation that your question creates:

- What would change? And why?
- What would decline?
- What would improve?
- How would you (or others) be affected?
- How would things be affected?
- How would procedures be affected?
- How would the organization be affected?
- How would equipment be affected?
- What would you (or others) do?
- What wouldn't you (or others) do?

To experiment with this, answer the question:

"What if...automobiles were outlawed in the Chicago city limits?"

There is another use of this technique that is extremely valuable. Periodically ask yourself, "What if...today was my first day on the job?" What would change?

This is valuable because it gives us the opportunity to see things that we should change, but haven't done so due to laziness or lack of discipline.

Remember back to the first day you started working for your current employer. During the course of that day, and several others to follow, I would wager that you saw a number of things you felt should have been done differently, better, or not at all.

Since you are no fool, you didn't immediately mention these observations. During your first few days on any job you aren't sure how to positively initiate changes, nor through whom to initiate them. More importantly, you don't know who to avoid when change is required.

So you sit back and mark time until you know enough to make the moves. Unfortunately, you are also learning to live with these perceived inequities. After all, you reason, if it's been done this way for all the years before you got here, certainly it can't hurt to leave it alone. Besides, you continue, these changes aren't worth upsetting the apple-cart. So you don't make the changes.

By asking the question, "What if today was the first day on the job; what would I change?" we have the ability to look at the job through our eyes when we were new to the task, with the insights that this perspective offers. In addition, we have our current level of experience to tell us how we must actually make the changes within the restraints of the organization.

I have never asked myself this question without it leading to constructive change in my area of responsibility. Try it tomorrow, you'll be amazed the insights it provides.

Why Not?

Another, more direct method of forcing new perspectives is the ability to ask irreverent or irrelevant questions. The answers to these questions force respondents to verbally justify their thinking.

Since childhood, we have been directly or subtly punished for asking questions that are either too direct or do not reflect well on our intelligence. Each of us can relate to the question we asked which elicited that unmistakable eyeball roll meant to imply infinite patience from the respondent.

It takes only a few of these occurrences to teach us the wisdom of cautious questioning. That is unfortunate, for it leaves only the children with a seemingly insatiable number of questions. As adults, that obvious curiosity has been dulled by the need to always appear intelligent.

Asking "Why?" or "Why not?" at seemingly inappropriate times forces the respondent to verbally substantiate their position. Those of us who have asked these questions know that such substantiation is not at all assured.

Begin by asking these two questions of yourself to become comfortable with potential responses. To really spur your thinking, the questions and the responses must be asked out loud. Doing this exercise in your head will serve only to justify your current thinking.

Mind Expansion Exercises

1. As the owner of a small business, you have to reduce personnel expenses by 40%. Understanding that putting aside rules can help inspire innovative ideas, you decide to give this unattractive task some concentrated effort. Make a list of ways you could reduce your personnel expenses by 40%, with as many options as possible which disregard any applicable rules.

2. Answer the question, "What if...I was the most competent professional in my field?"

3. Answer the question, "How could I verify my value to my employer if he found a machine to do my work for me?"

For potential approaches to the above problems, refer to the "Possibilities" section at the end of this book.

Chapter Six:
A Change in Perspective Helps

SUMMARY OF CHAPTER FIVE:

1. Our respect for the law, in its many forms, provides yet another barrier to our mental flexibility. If we can begin thinking about a problem or situation without our consideration of legal limits, we are able to perceive many new alternative approaches.
2. Asking questions provides the basic foundation for everything we know. The value of asking questions is no less in creativity. Asking the question "What if..." provides the element of fantasy in our thought processes and opens us up to new possibilities. The questions "Why?" or "Why not?" spur us and the respondents to verbally justify our position or ideas. Many ideas that are left unchallenged are also indefensible. Both of these questioning devices "fool" our mind into seeing new perspectives.

OBJECTIVES OF CHAPTER SIX:

1. Our current position relative to a problem or opportunity defines the way we perceive it and, in turn, where we are likely to look for solutions. By changing our perceived relationship to the situation, we can force ourselves to see new optimal solutions.

2. The several different entry points we can use in reviewing a situation will be listed, along with suggestions on how to use them profitably.

The Way We View Problems or Situations

The same acquired discipline that causes us to pursue commuter traffic, rather than off-road, thinking also affects the manner in which we store and access information in our brain. If we continue to always retrieve information from our mind in the same way, we are likely to always come up with the same solutions.

While reading the previous chapters, you have likely come to the conclusion that one of the keys to creative thinking is the ability to look at situations differently. This ability isn't just important in learning to think creatively, it is paramount.

There are very few ideas that will be historically verified as truly creative. Such an idea would be one that was initiated with no historical information base. As we know, every meaningful idea has been developed from information previously held.

If all of our innovative ideas are based on existing knowledge, why don't we all produce a steady stream of creative suggestions? The answer to this lies in the way information is stored in our head, and the manner in which we access that information.

Our memory is organized into bits of information, all categorized by subject. This organization is similar to the card file at your public library, where all books are listed by subject or author. If you want to access any of these books, you need only refer to a particular section of the library and secure the volume you want. If you were interested in baseball statistics, you wouldn't go to the section of the library that had information on climatic conditions in Greece.

This is precisely what makes creativity such a difficult

subject to learn and apply. To spur creativity, we are actually encouraging you to deliberately go into your brain and ask for information on the climatic conditions in Greece, hoping to find insights into baseball statistics!

Let me give you a simple example. I have been involved in advertising all of my professional life. As a result, I have in my brain a relatively substantial store of information; or a volume of books, if you will, on that subject. For roughly that same stretch of time, I have also been a parent of three children. This experience has given me an equally large (albeit inadequate) store of information on raising children.

If I am charged with the responsibility of developing an advertising campaign, I will instinctively go to that part of my brain that contains advertising knowledge. When I tap into that knowledge, I have the ability to put together a palatable, and hopefully successful, campaign.

If, however, I am hoping to develop a genuinely creative campaign, my chances of doing so are better if I go into the child-rearing (or other) part of my brain, rather than the advertising part of my brain. It is the mixing of information that gives creative insights.

By using information not related to advertising, I improve the chances of securing unique insights into my promotional efforts. This ability to mix information and view things from another direction is the key to success in creative thinking.

A profession that has used different-direction thinking to its advantage for years is the profession of comedy. The comedian tells you a story which you believe will lead in one direction, only to have the punch-line come at you from another direction. Thus it is funny. The classic line, "Take my wife...please!" is a classic example of this.

How to Change Your Perspective

Suggesting that we view a problem from a fresh perspective is far easier to say than do. Changing your entry point is a result of playing games with your mind, or altering the base of your current views.

This technique bases its effectiveness on the disrupting nature of changing our mental direction or information base. The technique is called "Changing Entry Point."

Our perception of a problem or opportunity is dictated by our position relative to that problem or opportunity. Depending where we are in a problem, we tend to see solutions from our perspective, not that of another person. While this is only natural, it also limits us when it comes time to develop novel solutions.

An experience with a client verified the value of this approach to me. This client has a factory in the suburbs of Chicago. We have worked together for a number of years. I received a call from the president of the firm in early 1982, with a request for assistance. They had just completed the worst sales year in their history. This wasn't any real shock, since many of my manufacturing clients had exactly the same experience. The year had seen a recession, from which some never recovered.

Anxious to prevent another poor sales year in 1983, the president asked if I would moderate an all-day session with their marketing group, with the objective of developing a stronger marketing strategy for the following year. I looked forward to working with them again. The sales staff was sharp and spontaneous, and I knew the session would go well. Not only that, but this firm had their meetings at a beautiful resort in southern Wisconsin. The available recreation would make the day go faster.

Armed with their latest sales statistics and a general idea of how I wanted the session to go, we met bright and early at 8 a.m. I planned to open the session by explaining that we wanted their ideas on how the marketing effort could be improved in the coming year. From that point on, the group was to take control, and I would only direct them toward the more reasonable options.

After about twenty minutes, the group appeared drained of ideas. My mistake was in not appreciating the devastating impact this sales failure had on their perception of the problem. They had been fighting this situation for over a year, and understood its staying power much better than I did. My lack of insight had created a real problem. How were we going to get ideas when they were convinced that they had no ideas to give?

To solve our dilemma, we changed our entry point. As soon as it was apparent we were at full stop, I asked the group to discontinue their current line of thinking and play a game of fantasy with me. I asked them to imagine that we were all sitting in the best restaurant in Chicago. It was a Friday evening, and the first night of a weekend given to us by the company. The reason for this celebration was our having completed the best sales year the firm had ever experienced.

Now with the image of a strong sales year in mind, I asked the group to list the events that could have taken place to cause this success. They changed their entry point into the problem. For the last year, they had struggled to prevent a sales disaster that happened despite their best efforts. They had, for a solid year, looked at the problem from the same direction. My request forced them to view the same problem, but from another perspective. They were being asked to look at the problem from the perspective of a successful conclusion, not from the current perspective of a stubborn problem.

At the time I made the request, we had only six suggestions on how to improve performance. When the day was over, we had over 100 ideas that we could explore to increase sales. Of these, several were followed. Based on a simple application of this tool, sales for this firm grew substantially in 1983.

Where You Can Enter a Problem or Opportunity

The four entry points which follow all provide a simple means of seeing problems from a new perspective.

To help you apply this valuable technique, four approaches are listed below.

Entering at a Positive Conclusion

The example above is one of entering at a positive conclusion. We suggested that the salespeople ignore the problem, and assume instead that we have a successful conclusion. Once we list all the possible events that could explain a successful conclusion, we then review those possibilities and identify the ones that we can execute now.

Legislating a Solution

With this approach, we ask ourselves, "If I could place myself at a point in time before this situation ever happened, what could I do to prevent its occurrence?" In effect, we assume we have the opportunity to make rules to prevent an unattractive occurrence. If we have the capacity to anticipate a future problem or opportunity, we certainly can make rules or create greater flexibilities to provide for it. You take a step back from the problem, assume that it isn't there, and plan to prevent it in the future. In the course of your "future planning" you likely derive solutions that may still be executed after the problem has occurred.

As an example, assume we are having problems with our teenager. To develop alternative solutions to this problem, we decide to use the technique of legislation. We assume our offspring has just been born. Recognizing that some day we might have discipline problems with our newly-configured bundle of noise, we establish limits and flexibilities now that will hopefully handle the discipline problems before they arise.

In doing so, we initiate the following:

1. We will advocate and reward complete honesty, on our part as well as that of our offspring.
2. A system will be set up whereby certain behaviors will increase our child's flexibility, and others will reduce it.
3. After a certain age, rules will be set by consensus, rather than dictated.

Under ideal circumstances, these legislated moves would improve the situation. While current conditions certainly are not ideal, the above suggestions could, at least partially, be initiated now.

Visualizing the "Perfect" Answer

This is a very simple technique for seeing possibilities that might be otherwise difficult to imagine. It is particularly effective in reviewing new products or improvements in existing products. With this technique, you simply look at a product or visualize it and say, "This product (situation, company, person, etc.) is perfect because it..." and describe what it is that makes it perfect.

In doing this with groups we use a safety razor as an example. Asking a group to describe a "perfect" safety razor generates product characteristics that might include:

- It jumps into your hand in the morning.

(Not particularly useful, but might lead to a better handle for the razor.)

- It lasts forever.

(Could lead to razors that could be resharpened.)

- It is available free.

(Not a popular idea with the accountants.)

- It doesn't need shaving cream; it enables the user to shave only every other day; etc.

Looking at the Problem Through the Eyes of Someone Else

If one of the problems we have in generating creative ideas is that we're stuck with a fixed background, wouldn't it be a good idea to "adopt" the background of someone else? While it may seem difficult to do, we can approach this level of flexibility with a little practice. How would a person with a different background see this situation?

One of the problems we discussed earlier in the book is that of being so close to our situation that it is difficult to see a new solution. It is this characteristic that makes us so much better at solving the problems of others than we are at solving our own. If we can develop our ability to look at our problems through the eyes of someone else, we will build the distance needed between the problem and ourselves to spur unique ideas.

Several years ago, I volunteered to work with the congregation of a local church to find a means of increasing membership. At one point in the session, I divided the participants into groups of five each. Each group was to assume the identity of a different person, i.e. the Pope, an industrialist, a student, a dentist, etc.

Using these identities, each group was then asked to generate as many membership increasing ideas as they could. Not only were the number of ideas impressive, but due to the different background identities assumed by the groups, the breadth of ideas was equally impressive.

Each of the above techniques can be used to help us

get into our problem from another direction. The value of this is that it enables us to break away from our preconceived notions concerning a situation or problem.

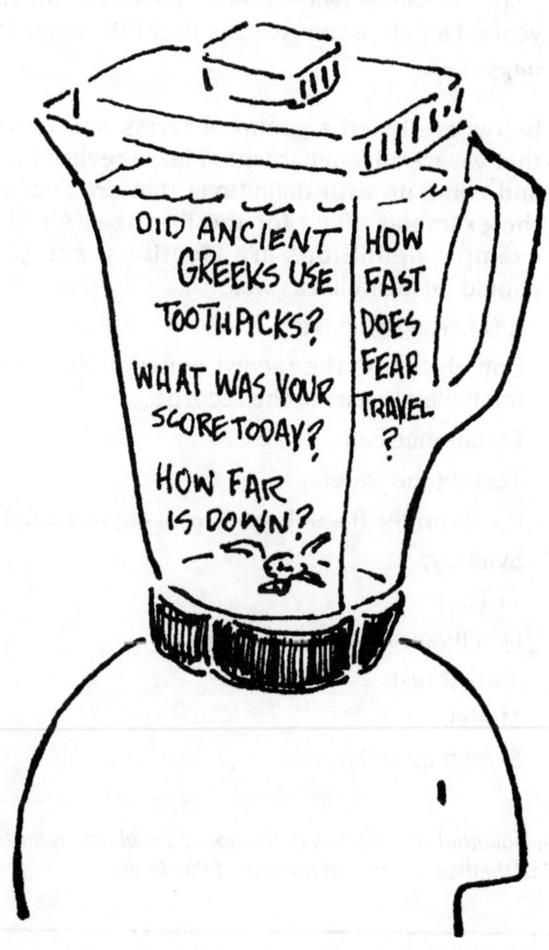

Mind Expansion Exercises

1. For the last six years your car dealership has offered a spring inventory reduction sale. This year, the sale is twice as effective as the previous years. List all of the reasons that this might have happened.

2. Below are listed a group of terms and phrases that we are all familiar with. Please review the list and come up with definitions that are similar to the examples given for the first few. All of the example definitions are facetious, and yours should be facetious as well.

   R.O.I.: rolling on ice

   Confab: an off-the-record conversation that is immediately part of the record

   Conference call:

   Testing the water:

   Run it up the flagpole and see if anyone salutes:

   Synergy:

   J.I.T.:

   Quality circles:

   Market test:

   Model:

   Screening calls:

For potential approaches to the above problems, refer to the "Possibilities" section at the end of this book.

Chapter Seven:

Redefining Your Way to Creativity

SUMMARY OF CHAPTER 6:

1. Our mental flexibility, or creativity, is substantially affected by our position relative to a problem or situation. By changing this initial position or "entry point," we can materially increase the likelihood of innovative thinking.
2. Four simple entry point changes include:
   - Entering at a positive conclusion
   - Legislating a solution
   - Visualizing the "perfect" answer
   - Looking at the problem through the eyes of someone else

OBJECTIVES OF CHAPTER 7:

1. The role of definition and its impact on our creativity will constitute the major share of this chapter. By modifying the definition of the situation or problem, we can open ourselves to perspectives we might not otherwise have pursued.
2. If we accept a limited definition of a problem or situation, we also will limit the number of perceived solutions. This relationship will be developed in this chapter. We will also offer a means of broadening our problem, or opportunity, definitions.

ARE YOU TOO SHORT OR ARE YOUR FRIENDS TOO TALL?

The way we perceive ourselves to a large extent dictates the limits within which we operate. Psychologists and sociologists have both shown us that if we have positive feelings or if we define ourselves in a positive way, we tend to act more positively and reap more positive life experiences as a result.

The concept of seeing ourselves as winners or losers and its impact on our success is basically one of definition. Therefore, if we can doctor the definition of ourselves to see ourselves in a more positive (or innovative) light, then we will act in a manner to reinforce that self-image.

On the negative side of this is the concept of the self-fulfilling prophecy. This suggests that when people are given negative information about something, they tend to follow through on the negative, even in the face of positive input. In one instance, teachers were told that a class they were to begin teaching was populated with some inferior students. At the end of the semester these students received average or below average grades, despite the fact that they were actually in the higher I.Q. range.

Similarly, when teachers were advised that their future class was comprised of certain gifted students, these students received above average grades at the end of the semester, despite the fact that they were of average ability.

The reason these students responded to their teachers' expectations of them is not that test scores were juggled or student educational needs ignored. They responded to the teachers' expectations because the teachers, from a position of respect and authority, had established a goal they felt was reasonable for the student. The student responded to that goal, as it impacted their perceptions of themselves.

In this same category is the use of visualization in improving the performance of athletes. A number of training videotapes are available which encourage visualizing for skill reinforcement. Skiers are encouraged to "see" themselves negotiating a difficult turn, basketball players are taught to "visualize" the ball going through the hoop. All of these examples deal with operating from a defined position of success.

How Definitions Limit or Expand Our Perceptions

When we accept a specific definition of a problem or situation, we accept also the parameters that come with that definition. If we change the definition, we then change the parameters. The result will be increased mental flexibility.

In the history of American business, the impact of definition has been clearly identified. Few marketing texts leave out the story of the American railroads and the role definition played in their success. In the late 1800's, the railroad industry was the darling of the rapidly industrialized United States. Railroads were the most economical means of moving goods for a growing industrial nation. Their expansion and wealth had attracted investors from the monarchies of Europe. Any right-thinking financial analyst had to agree that their influence would spread throughout the 20th century.

At that time, if you had asked a railroad executive how he defined his business, he would have proudly indicated that he was in the *railroad* business. At that time, this definition would have been seen only as harmless shortsightedness on his part. Later, this shortsightedness would virtually destroy that industry.

As competitors entered the transportation industry, this same railroad executive continued to identify his economic contribution as being the railroad industry. At the time that cars and trucks became more common in the United States, the rail industry stagnated. Also at that time, one of the few industries that had the financial resources to enter the growing markets for automobiles and trucks was railroads. By using the restricted definition of the railroad industry, they never saw the opportunities provided by the transportation industry.

Had they seen themselves as competitors in *transportation* rather than just *rail*, they could have justified entering the automobile and truck markets, perhaps even air transportation as well. Not only are we not driving Illinois Central automobiles, we're not flying to Florida this winter aboard Union Pacific airplanes. We could be, if the management of railroad firms had been far-sighted enough to define their industry in broader terms.

Today the financial condition of railroads is well known and not envied. Government intervention saved many of these former giants from complete collapse. Rails have been removed by the mile, and only recently has this downward trend been reversed.

Nor is the railroad example unique. When television was introduced in the late 1940's, Hollywood studios saw its presence as a threat. They tried everything they could think of to blackball entertainers who performed on television, and generally would have nothing to do with this new medium. Like the railroads, they defined their domain in too narrow a fashion. They saw themselves as being in the *movie* business, rather than in the broader *entertainment* business. If they had seen themselves in the entertainment business, they would properly have seen television as a means to expand their influence, rather than as a competitor.

Redefining Your Way to Creative Ideas

If definition plays such a significant role in perceptions, can we modify our perceptions by simply redefining a situation? This tool is not only simple, but it also provides a broad base with which to expand our thinking.

Redefinition is a useful tool in creativity. Earlier, we saw how a friend has used redefinition to solve the problem of high employee turnover. He had redefined that problem as "people leaving the plant." To solve the problem of "people leaving the plant," he had suggested tying their legs together.

This redefinition had opened his mind and the mind of others around him. Based on that new perspective, a solution was found, where the solution had been elusive with other means of looking at the problem. Where he could not find a solution to the "turnover" problem, he certainly could solve the problem of "people leaving the plant."

Redefinition is a means of breaking out of a tunnel vision relative to a problem or opportunity. We frequently dwell on a problem for so long that we aren't able to change our perspective. Sometimes the best way to relieve that blockage is to change slightly the definition of the problem, and then provide solutions for the new definition.

In the formative years of American participation in international sports car racing, an American from Texas named Jim Hall built and raced a stable of race cars named the "Chaparral." Jim Hall was sufficiently new in international sports car racing to be a true innovator.

At one point in his career he introduced a car to the competition that was quickly nicknamed the "vacuum cleaner." To improve the handling of the car, Hall installed an auxiliary motor on his car that powered a huge fan. He skirted the bottom of the car with a fabric material to reduce air leakage. When the auxiliary fan was turned on, it actually "sucked" the car to the surface of the track, substantially increasing the car's ability to handle high-speed turns.

Perhaps Jim Hall had redefined "improved handling" to "stay on the road," which could have led to "stick to the road," which in turn might have led to the idea of the "vacuum cleaner" sports car.

If you are at all interested in why this excellent idea isn't being used today, ask yourself, "What happens to revolutionary ideas in a static organization?" You guessed it. The concept was banned by the sanctioning body of sports car racing.

The technique of redefinition is less commuter traffic and more off-road than the other techniques we have discussed. It requires a bit more mental flexibility on our part than other techniques. There are three basic methods of using redefinition: the abbreviated redefinition, the multiple redefinition, and the detailed redefinition.

The Abbreviated Redefinition

The first application of redefinition is to shorten the definition to as few words as possible, preferably two. The problem of poor marketing performance, in its shortest form, would be "low sales." In the case of my friend and his situation of high employee turnover, the problem would be defined simply as "employee turnover," "disloyal employees," or "employee selection."

The value of this abbreviated interpretation is that it supplies so little information on the problem that it tends to permit a broader range of solutions when looking for alternatives.

The Multiple Redefinition

The second way to use the technique of redefinition is to list as many different definitions of the problem as you can. Each of the redefinitions should say roughly the same thing, but in different terms. For instance, if our problem is "too much paperwork," then our redefinitions might be rewritten to include:

- Too many internal memos
- Too much correspondence
- Inadequate storage
- Too many customers
- Too many employees
- Procedures too complicated
- Too many communication channels
- Too much information
- Too many reproductions of information
- Too many people in the loop
- Too much work
- Too much writing

Each of these redefinitions suggests a different type of solution. For instance, if the problem is defined as "inadequate storage," this suggests a very different type of solution than the definition "procedures too complicated." Each time we redefine the problem, we should see different types of possible solutions.

The Detailed Redefinition

The last way to use this technique is to redefine the problem in as much detail as possible. This is a direct contradiction to our initial use of this technique, where we shortened the definition. With this approach, we try to put as much detail into the definition as we possibly can. The purposes of doing this is to see if we can enter the problem at a different location in the detailed problem definition, each potential location provided by the detailed information contained in the definition.

Several years ago, a participant at my creativity workshop used this approach to solve a problem he had struggled with for some time. He had identified his problem as

"I have too little personal time." When we came to this point in the workshop, he decided to use this approach to find a solution to that problem. His lengthened definition was:

> *"I find that in the course of my 16 hour day, the demands on my time of my job, family, commuting, personal hygiene, and eating are such that I have too few hours for activities which I consider recreational or personal."*

This lengthened definition provided several new insights for this individual. In the first line, he identified his day as consisting of 16 hours. When we discussed this, he indicated that before he wrote this down, he had always felt that the part of the day he controlled was only 8 hours long. In redefining the problem, it was apparent to him that the part of his day that was within his control was clearly 16 hours, rather than 8.

He also found in his lengthened definition he had listed some demands on his time that could well be considered recreational, such as eating or family time. Was he, he asked, properly using these hours as recreation or was he seeing them as a burden instead? The comment "too few hours" also caught his attention. How many hours were "too few?" He realized he had never established a number of hours which would be considered adequate. Would it take five? Or would two be enough?

By broadening his original definition, this participant was able to see his problem in a different light and also see new solutions based on that insight.

For your information, the definition he used for his analysis was not particularly long. Many of my participants find that they can easily write several pages of redefinition for their review. This should be your objective as well.

Mind Expansion Exercises

1. How many different definitions can you identify for the problem of:

   •"Poor sales performance"

   •"Out-of-control budget"

   •"Our people don't see how they will benefit"

2. Refer to the above three situations and redefine these problems using as long a definition as possible. You will have to add, or assume, additional information to do this.

3. Redefine one of the problems you listed for yourself in Chapter Two.

For potential approaches to the above problems, refer to the "Possibilities" section at the end of this book.

Chapter Eight:

Using Structure to Take Structure Out of Your Thinking

SUMMARY OF CHAPTER 7:

There is a strong relationship between the alternative solutions we recommend, and the definition of the problem or situation as we initially perceive it. To take best advantage of this, we discussed shortening the definition, lengthening the definition, and creating multiple definitions to give us better insights into potential solutions. With each redefinition, we expose ourselves to new perspectives of the problem, and therefore new solutions as well.

OBJECTIVE OF CHAPTER 8:

Many people operate best when they have a firm structure to help organize their thoughts or work. This chapter offers a technique that is best at providing this structured setting. Referred to as forced multiples, this method helps us see pieces of the puzzle without getting lost in the entire structure.

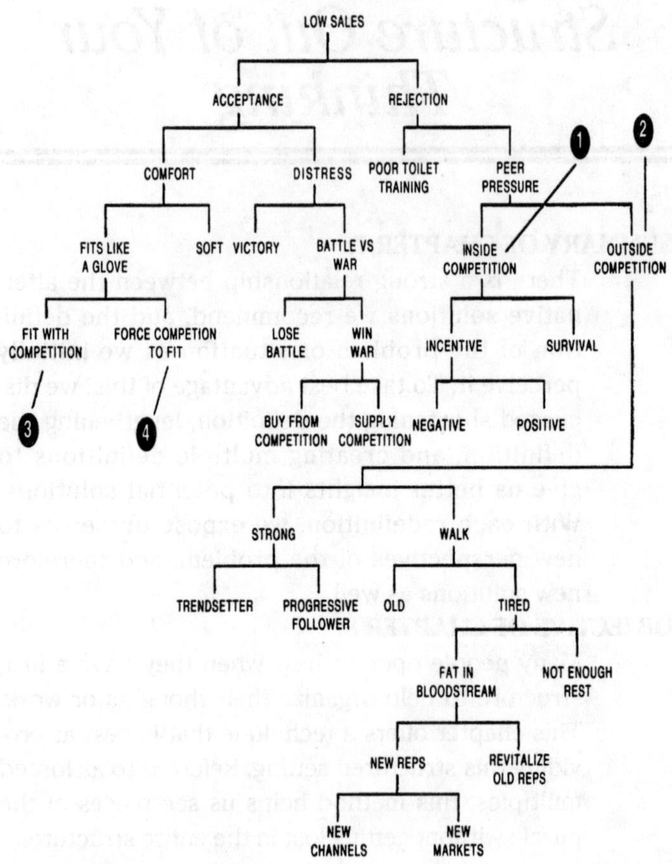
Forced Multiples
LOW SALES
ACCEPTANCE
REJECTION
COMFORT
DISTRESS
POOR TOILET TRAINING
PEER PRESSURE
1
2
FITS LIKE A GLOVE
SOFT
VICTORY
BATTLE VS WAR
INSIDE COMPETITION
OUTSIDE COMPETITION
FIT WITH COMPETITION
FORCE COMPETION TO FIT
LOSE BATTLE
WIN WAR
INCENTIVE
SURVIVAL
3
4
BUY FROM COMPETITION
SUPPLY COMPETITION
NEGATIVE
POSITIVE
STRONG
WALK
TRENDSETTER
PROGRESSIVE FOLLOWER
OLD
TIRED
FAT IN BLOODSTREAM
NOT ENOUGH REST
NEW REPS
REVITALIZE OLD REPS
NEW CHANNELS
NEW MARKETS

The Technique of Forced Multiples

Forced multiples, as an idea-generating tool, offer a number of attractive traits. It is simple to understand, overcomes one of the major barriers to innovative thinking, and is suitable for a disciplined approach to creativity.

The technique of forced multiples is ideal for the disciplined creative thinker—the person who prefers structure, even in their creativity.

Studies verify that each of us learns differently. Some learn through visual means, others by reading or audial approaches. Similarly, some people prefer discipline in their learning experiences, while others respond better if given a free hand. Surprisingly, even in the process of learning something as resistant to structure as creativity, some people are more comfortable learning this skill through a specific and precise means.

While forced multiples is basically simple, it is easier to show than explain. On the opposite page is a forced multiples example which was used with a client firm a few years ago. The client had asked for some help in developing options in their marketing effort. They manufactured a large piece of metal fabricating equipment, so large that each of their products weighed about six tons apiece.

This firm was suffering inroads from foreign competitors, as was just about everyone at that time. Two firms in particular, one each from Italy and Germany, had proven to be especially nettlesome. This forced multiples tree is a result of the firm's officers working to develop new marketing approaches. Follow the steps we pursued on the forced multiples tree above.

At the start, each forced multiples tree has a problem statement, or a statement about the problem. At the top center of the tree is the statement "low sales." The next rung down is divided into "acceptance" and "rejection."

Why those two categories were chosen is not particularly important. The only criterion is that every branch be divided into at least two sub-branches. The two needn't complement, contradict, or relate to one another. The only requirement is that we continue dividing ideas into subideas until our thinking dries up in that area. We then move to another branch of the tree and repeat the process.

The idea behind the development of a forced multiples tree is simple; you need only start with the statement of the problem or about the problem. Then develop the branches under that statement in units of at least two at a time. You needn't follow any predetermined pattern, nor divide ideas into any set categories. Simply list the first things that come to mind. As you can see from the tree my client developed, sometimes branches go nowhere, particularly the "poor toilet training" example. That division just came into their minds, so they wrote it down.

A caution is appropriate here. We have suggested that the starting point of a forced multiples tree should be a statement of the problem, or about the problem. The natural tendency would be to list potential solutions under that starting point. If you attempt to do this, you will likely short-circuit your entire creative effort.

Under the starting point list general and casual extensions. If you get into solutions now, you reduce the likelihood that other solutions will come to your mind.

This tree was used to benefit my client in the following manner. After all of the people involved in the project had developed their own tree, each was passed to other group members to encourage different interpretations of the branches.

To enhance your understanding of their conclusions, we have numbered those branches of the forced multiples tree which led to new insights.

Numbers one and two provided fresh input. We were

aware that the company was well established as a competitor to outside firms, but little or nothing had been done to foster competition between individuals or departments within the company. This was worth looking into.

Similarly, numbers three and four also triggered productive responses. The piece of equipment manufactured by the client was generally competitive with others, but failed to compete in terms of the numerically controlled "brain" offered by the competitors. The hardware portion was excellent. Looking at one of the trees, one executive observed that for all but 100 pounds of their equipment, they should be leaders in the industry. This was followed by the observation that the competition would be really fierce if the competitors found a domestic supplier for their hardware. This observation was triggered by the entry "fit with competition."

After a few moments, the president of the firm offered, "Unless that domestic supplier was us." The thought sank in for a few minutes before anything was said. Despite the lessened appeal of producing hardware for a competitor, there certainly were some attractive elements of the proposal. The firm could place itself in a position to be part of a larger market, with a broader market base.

After weeks of consideration, each of the foreign competitors was approached with the idea. The competitor that was the most attractive to my client was interested and a relationship was established.

In someone's eyes, the "fit with competition" and "force competition to fit" looked like a cooperative venture. After some months, that is exactly what it was—to the benefit of the firm.

The purpose of forced multiples is, as its title implies, to force us into thinking in multiples. We have previously discussed our tendency of looking for only one answer. This technique insists that we pursue at least two avenues at a time. If an avenue doesn't inspire original or beneficial thinking, we can stop and continue working to subdivide other branches. The secret of the technique is to let your thinking proceed without a pattern, and then review what you have listed to look for new inroads. In the example above, it took one individual to see the benefit of the branches, and another to interpret the benefit.

With some practice, these trees can be huge. Also, after developing the tree, you will frequently find new ideas if you review the tree again several days after its origination.

A caution about the use of forced multiples. Notice the tree doesn't start with a functional division of ideas. We didn't try to subdivide branches into customer types, market channels, or other similarly functional splits. If you begin this technique with functional divisions, you'll find that your flexibility is limited. Begin instead with simple observations or comments about the problem statement. If it is still a challenge for you, make the problem statement less specific. Remember, you are trying to be less specific with this technique.

The Benefit of Merging Techniques

There are few absolutes to deal with in learning to think more creatively. Any method that we use to generate new ideas is acceptable if it works for us. Similarly, we may also find a benefit in combining two or more methods.

One of the pleasures of working in creativity is the basic lack of rules to go by. This lack of rules gives us the opportunity to merge techniques if it will help us think more flexibly. For instance, it was suggested above that we break each branch into sub-branches, until we can't think of any more divisions. In Chapter Seven we talked about using redefinition to prompt creative ideas. We can also use redefinition to help us be more effective in using forced multiples as well.

For instance, in the previous example of the forced multiples tree there were several branches that did not lead to interesting or beneficial sub-branches. Going back to those fruitless ideas, we redefine them, and start over again. For instance, refer to "poor toilet training." If we redefine this to read "loose discipline," immediately "tighter controls" and "motivation" are seen as likely entries. With this redefinition, we're off and running again!

The combining of techniques is something you will develop with a little practice. The forced multiples tree is an excellent starting point for this cross-fertilization. You will find that some of your entries will be enriched by redefining, as we have already seen. In addition, you'll also see that some of your entries are excellent *entry points* for looking at the problem or situation from another direction.

Don't let any of the instructions we offer limit your thinking. Break any rule or suggestion you wish if it helps you see things differently.

MULTIPLE OPTIONS ☛ NEW APPROACHES

REDEFINITIONS

Mind Expansion Exercises

1. Develop a forced multiples tree for these situations:

   - Inventory too low to sustain full production
   - Cutting tools aren't sufficiently durable
   - (Substitute one of your three problems listed in Chapter Two)

2. Use the forced multiples tree to come up with names for the following new products:

   - A mass transit system that offers accommodations for only one or two people in each vehicle, but will take its passengers from their doorstep to their destination.
   - Shoes that are attractive enough for dress occasions, yet are built, and are comfortable enough, for cross-training.
   - A line of dairy products that needs no refrigeration.
   - An executive desk that offers a slanted top to enhance paperwork.

For potential approaches to the above problems, refer to the "Possibilities" section at the end of this book.

Chapter Nine:

Moving the Immobile: The Number Juggle

SUMMARY OF CHAPTER 8:

1. Forced multiples is a means of generating creative ideas within a disciplined environment. The success of this technique is based on forcing us to see multiple directions for each of our ideas.
2. The flexibility built into our creative thinking techniques can be used to combine diverse techniques for new ideas. We combined forced multiples and redefinition in the example in Chapter Eight.

OBJECTIVE OF CHAPTER 9:

Numeric relationships have provided the basis for some of mankind's most innovative breakthroughs. This is startling, especially when we consider how inflexible numbers appear. This chapter will demonstrate a means of using numbers to generate creative ideas. Through a form of "numeric deception," artificial values will be assigned to elements of our problem, and then used to force fresh perspectives.

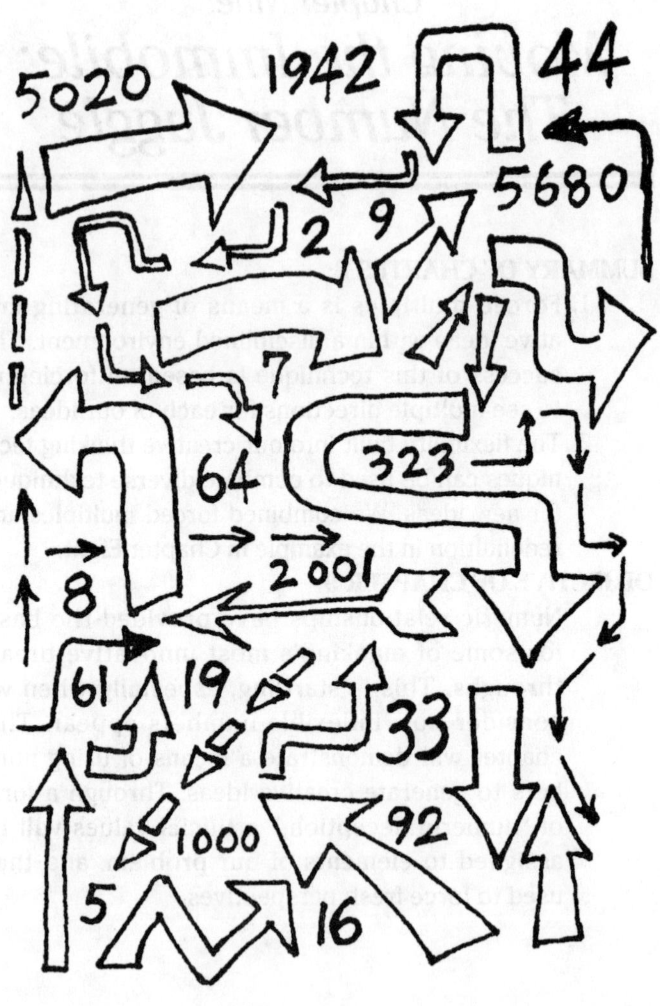
5020
1942
44
5680
9
2
7
323
64
2001
8
61
19
33
92
1000
5
16

Nothing has advanced the concept of logical thought like the development of the number system. Virtually all of the scientific principles with which we are familiar are a product of it. The laws of physics are expressed in numeric terms, as are the relationships of the planets and atomic weights.

Numbers help us understand distances, time and statistical concepts. Even the inexact sciences of sociology, psychology and marketing strive to add credence to their respective professions by forcing numeric relationships to describe the behavior of people. In many cases these numeric relationships help us to understand and predict behavior patterns of groups.

Despite its strengths, the numeric system is not generally friendly to creative thinking. There is a simple explanation for this: numeric thinking gives the appearance of total inflexibility. Total inflexibility is, as we already know, not a good environment for creative thought.

This isn't much of a problem normally, as numbers tend to be important only in situations that can be easily measured. However, the very existence of numbers in a problem or opportunity tend to discourage whatever opportunity for creativity that may exist. We have already seen an example (what is half of 13?) where apparent inflexibility can actually be an opportunity for innovative thinking. There is a tendency to accept the notion of "what is, is" when we see numbers. It's too bad we don't have as much regard for our creativity as we do for our learned discipline!

The Number Juggle

If we can force flexibility into the way we see numbers, we can imply artificially broad boundaries into our perceptions of a problem. These new boundaries enable us to look for fresh alternatives.

To counteract the tendency to throw up our hands in surrender when faced with the apparent inflexibility of numbers, we recommend a technique called the *number juggle*. Like redefinition, this is not a complicated technique, but it does take some practice to use effectively.

Also like redefinition, this is a multi-step technique. In the first step, you need to identify everything in your problem or opportunity that can be explained in terms of numbers or can be measured. In the previous problem of "low sales," this was no problem. Here numbers were easily attached to: sales dollars, number of customers, number of products, number of distribution outlets, number of salespeople, average dollar per transaction, etc.

Other problems are not as obviously described by numbers. For instance, the problems of "low morale," "poor styling," or "inadequate communication" are less easily put into numeric terms. More difficult; but certainly not impossible.

In the second step of the "number juggle," we increase, decrease, multiply, subtract, transpose and otherwise juggle the numeric relationships. After doing this, we review these artificially derived numbers and try to identify their impact on our situation.

The easiest way to understand this technique is through an example. Assume that we are the parents of three teenaged children. We both work, and the kids are involved in a host of after-school activities and cannot always be relied on to be home in time for dinner. We'd be more angry about that if, in fact, we were any better about being home on time. Sometimes we have to work late, to entertain a client, or to wrap up a project after work.

The end result is that there is no time for the entire family to sit down for a meal and enjoy the company of each other. Our experiments to solve the problem have failed, normally with the result of anger on someone's part for the failed attempt. Our problem is, how can we all sit down to a meal each day as a family?

Remembering step one, we start by identifying all the numbers in our problem. The numbers in this situation aren't particularly obvious, but we're able to generate the following list, which includes:

- Number of people in the family (five).
- Number of meals per day, or week (three or 21).
- Number of food preparers (normally one).
- Number of activities in which the family members participate (infinite).
- Number of people at each meal (average four).
- Number of courses per meal (average two).
- Number of locations where meals are possible (infinite).
- Number of dollars available to solve the problem (?).

There are certainly more opportunities to attach numbers to this situation, but we should have enough to start. By reviewing and modifying these numbers we hope to trigger some unique ideas.

Number of people in the family

There are five of us. If there were ten, the problem would be worse, and would probably require military-type preparation for family meals. Do we need military discipline? If there were only two of us, we could eat every meal out at a mutually convenient location. Would everyone show up at a restaurant? (Notice that by juggling the numbers, we are giving ourselves a different perspective of the problem.)

Number of meals per day

Instead of three, what if there were 15, one for each

member of the family? What if there were only one? If there were only one, which meal would be the easiest to coordinate? (Interesting, if you and I are thinking alike, you probably were thinking that the evening meal was the meal in question. Wouldn't breakfast be the most reasonable meal to coordinate?)

Number of food preparers

This doesn't seem central to our problem, as the preparer must be at the meal. What if one of the kids had to help prepare every meal? That would certainly assure one of them being present. They likely would put pressure on other family members to show up as well, not wanting their efforts to go unnoticed. What if there were no preparers? That could mean we'd eat out all the time. Not attractive, but certainly an option on occasion. (Ideas have been generated here by both expanding and contracting the numbers.)

Number of activities

Too many! What would the impact be of having twice this number of activities? The only way we'd get the family to show up for a meal would be to make the meal itself an activity. Maybe we could do that. It would require expanding the involvement (i.e., everyone gets to play!). What would the impact be of having no outside activities? Probably none. We're active people, and we'd fill any voids with some form of activity. I don't think that reducing activities is a realistic option.

Number of people at each meal

This is the crux of the problem. The number should be five, but is only four on average. If the number was substantially reduced, say to two or three, not enough people in the family would care. This would make it a "nonproblem." If we increased the number of people at the meal to seven, we'd have to invite outsiders to attend the meal. This doesn't sound really attractive. If we did invite someone to the meal, however, it would increase the likelihood of attendance. Everyone responds differently to a meal when guests are invited.

Number of courses per meal

If we limited the number of courses to one, it would certainly meet with our approval, but likely no one else's. If we expanded the number of courses, it would make the meal better at the price of our fragile disposition. Still, it might be worth considering.

Number of locations where meals are possible.

This one keeps cropping up. It could be a real incentive for everyone to eat out at a mutually attractive location. There are probably 50 reasonable alternatives here.

Number of dollars available to solve this problem.

If we doubled, or for that matter halved, the money available, it likely wouldn't change the situation.

After reviewing the information we listed above, some alternative solutions become apparent. We decided that the best time during which to coordinate a "family meal" was, in fact, breakfast, not dinner as we had originally thought. Not only that, we discovered an invited guest would have a positive influence on attendance and mealtime demeanor. Also, the idea of multiple preparers had some distinct appeal.

The above situation was presented to me by a woman who attended one of my sessions on creativity some time ago. What follows is a result of her "number juggle."

She decided to insist that each weekday breakfast be prepared by one of the kids and one of the parents. It was to be no humble affair, as each breakfast was to consist of no less than three courses. In addition, a guest of one of the kids or parents would be asked to join the meal one day per week.

Initially, she had a difficult time selling everyone on the virtues of her plan. After all, two unfortunates were going to arise each morning by 5:30 to get the meal set up. After several weeks of seeing that she was serious, the family surrendered and the breakfast became an institution.

Not only was the plan a huge success, but there were also some residual benefits. Anyone who has raised children knows that after they reach puberty, you tend to see your offspring only under duress. This arrangement allowed for one parent and one offspring to spend an hour together about once a week. This represents a real communication breakthrough.

The technique of number juggling enables us to see situations in a much more flexible manner, even in cases where we don't think we have that option.

Mind Expansion Exercises

1. Identify the numbers hidden in these situations:

    - Poor morale among employees

    - An attitude problem in a department

    - A lack of "vision" on the part of your employees

2. Juggle the numbers you identified above, and see if potential solutions are suggested as a result.

For potential approaches to the above problems, refer to the "Possibilities" section at the end of this book.

Chapter Ten:

How to Relate the Unrelated

SUMMARY OF CHAPTER 9:

By impose false numeric values to the elements of our problem or situation, we broaden the boundaries within which we view our alternatives. These new boundaries permitted us to develop unique perspectives of our situation, and lead to fresh innovations.

OBJECTIVE OF CHAPTER 10:

By relating totally unrelated objects to our problem, we further press our innovative abilities. This extension of the "number juggle" goes a step farther in fantasy, and requires that we force two dissimilar objects together in an attempt to create innovative perspectives.

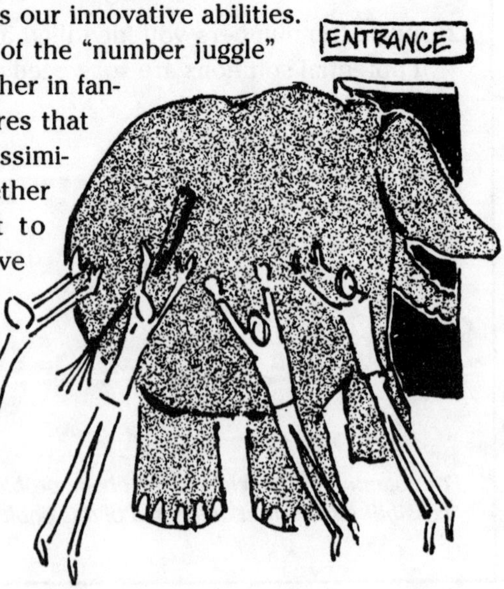

"If you know what you are looking for," the old saying goes, "you may find it, but you're not likely to find anything else." While the relevance of this phrase to creativity may not be immediately apparent, it is relevant nonetheless.

I have a good friend who travels as part of his work. While some of us are forced to spend time in sub-wonderful places, my friend seems to hit all the beautiful parts of the country. He is constantly referring to his latest trip to Colorado, Southern California or the Keys of Florida. Despite spending a reasonable amount of time in these beautiful places, he has seen none of the sights.

After returning from New York City, my friend hasn't seen a live Broadway play, been on the Staten Island Ferry, visited the Statue of Liberty, or walked through Central Park. If his latest trip was to Florida, I assure you that he couldn't take the time to see EPCOT® Center or Disney World.

His affliction is shared by a number of us. We can relate to the reasons these opportunities are lost. When business people travel to exotic sites, they aren't there to recreate. They are there to conduct business and often have a strict schedule to which they must adhere. If we travel to an interesting out-of-town location, we rarely spend any time on the local sights. Our purpose is to initiate contact with a firm, close a deal, and try to create some goodwill with a new account. We don't take the time to let the area soak in, and we do it on purpose.

In effect, "we know what we're looking for and we very well may find it, but we're not going to find anything else."

Forcing the Outside In

Much of creative thinking is based on serendipity, or a pleasant, unexpected outcome. In effect, many of the techniques and suggestions we have made thus far are designed to encourage serendipitous thinking. By using the technique of "Exposure," we again are pressing ourselves to achieve this benefit.

Looking only for things you hope to find is debilitating in your creative thinking. Because you are familiar with most of the circumstances surrounding your problems or opportunities, you learn to "anticipate" a correct response. You aren't really looking for new ideas or "scenery" anymore because you have the "correct answer" already in mind.

A foreman with whom I worked was being groomed for a future general management job. During a conversation with him, a section leader interrupted us and indicated that Machine 6 had broken its third cutting tool in the last two hours. The foreman exclaimed, "I should have fired that guy last week when this came up the first time." I am certainly no expert on the causes of cutting tool failure, but I do know that it can be caused by things in addition to operator error. The foreman, who obviously had dealt with this situation before, was prepared to act on the unsubstantiated notion that the operator was at fault. The foreman clearly wouldn't have spent any more time on the Staten Island Ferry than my busy friend.

The foreman might well be justified in his conclusion, but the point is that he had effectively stopped looking for other options.

How many times do we find ourselves in the same position—with our kids, jobs, friends, or strangers? We depend so much on our prior exposure to a situation, that we no longer entertain new information. Our next creativity technique is designed to prevent that. The technique is called *Exposure*.

Of all our techniques, exposure is likely the most OR (off-road) in its approach. To use it, we must force a relationship between our problem or situation and another totally unrelated object. After doing so, we then ask ourselves, "How are these two related?"

To begin this approach we identify an inanimate object and list all of its characteristics. It is easier to use a tree, due to its complex character. The terms we might include to describe a tree could be:

brown
bugs
shade
green
leaves
rake
home
birds
strong
old
bark
rough
alive
rigid
flexible
seasonal
beneficial
wood
paper

We now have a beginning list of the terms we would use to describe a tree. Now we can relate these terms to our problem and force a relationship between them.

Assume that we're bored with our job, but for several reasons we don't want to leave it now. Our problem is, "How can we relieve boredom on the job?" Looking to our list of tree characteristics, we compare each characteristic to our problem and look for a relationship.

Brown

How is this color like my problem? Dull? Earth tone? Life-giving? Dirt?

(I don't see anything here now.)

Bugs

Insects. Parasites. Eating the tree.

(What are my bugs? What is actually "eating my tree?" The tree doesn't always survive. Maybe I should identify my bugs before they remove the option of leaving my employer at my behest rather than theirs.)

Shade

Protection. Shelter. Shady. Undercover. Not fully exposed.

(I'm not being very direct about my attitude or feelings. Should I be? Do I relish the protection of the job more than I relish the opportunity to work elsewhere?)

Green

Money. Raw. No experience. Income. Photosynthesis.

Nourishment

(Is there a place where I can get the "nourishment" I am apparently lacking?)

-etc.

As you can see, our objective with exposure is to force similarities where none apparently exist. This exposure should be to a totally unrelated object. Exposure helps us resist the impulse to always have a solution at hand, and pressures us to see known situations from a different perspective.

You may find that using more than one object to summarize will be valuable in this technique. In the above example, if we identified the characteristics of a styrofoam cup as well as a tree, we'd find a completely different set of terms to trigger our thinking.

Mind Expansion Exercises

1. Take ten 3 x 5 cards and on each card write the name of an object—any object that comes to mind. At random, select any two and try to conjure what you could make from a combination of both of them.

   A. Mix up the cards and do this exercise repeatedly.

   B. Instead of using nondescript objects on your cards, use objects that relate to a problem or opportunity you currently face.

   C. Try this exercise with your kids. It not only is a lot of fun, but you will also find out how few restrictions they have in their thinking.

2. Take any two objects you use at work or at home and see what you can come up with by combining the two.

For potential approaches to the above problems, refer to the "Possibilities" section at the end of this book.

Chapter 11:

Your Daily Creativity Diet

SUMMARY OF CHAPTER 10:

Knowing that our perception of a situation provides inherent limitations to the number of solutions we can see, we used *exposure* to increase the number of possible alternatives. *Exposure* forces us to relate two unrelated objects, which serves to broaden our perception.

OBJECTIVE OF CHAPTER 11:

Change in our performance will not occur until there is a change in routine. We will suggest seven simple changes to your daily routine that will enhance your innovative abilities.

For those of you who have taken a speed-reading course, the following chain of events will likely ring a bell with you.

1. You take the course and practice the techniques that are recommended.
2. You're amazed that your reading speed does increase, and you exercise with more enthusiasm.
3. You develop even more speed, and surprisingly more comprehension as well.
4. You complete the course, flatter the instructor, and head home to revel in your new skill.

After several weeks, it occurs to you that some of the glitter has worn off your new skills. In fact, you seem to be reading at the same rate you did before you took the course. The reason? You hadn't made the use of the techniques for speed reading part of your daily routine, and as a result they were not turned into new reading habits.

This same thing will happen in your attempts to think more creatively, unless you adopt daily changes in the way you do things. The list of suggestions below are intended to help you keep a crisp mental outlook with a minimum of effort.

Change Your Morning Routine: Upset Your Homeostasis!

Each of us has a routine that we follow in the morning. Earlier in the book it was indicated that these routines are so well established that we really don't have to think at all before we get to work in the morning. Everything is done for us unconsciously.

During the time you are letting these routines run your activities, your mind is basically asleep. The sooner you wake it up in the morning, the sooner you can think about new things. For this reason we recommend that you do something different each morning. Nothing necessarily earth-shattering, just enough to get your mind started.

For instance, if you eat breakfast at home, eat out. If you follow a particular route to work, find another route. If you go to work alone, go with someone else. If you drive to work, take public transportation.

Do something different to help wake up your mind earlier in the day.

Analyze At Least One Problem Per Day

If we've learned nothing else from this book, we have learned that our education and experience can severely limit our creativity if we let them. All of the techniques we learned here are designed to prevent this in one form or another.

To help initiate the discipline of rethinking old habits, make it a practice to use one of the tools we presented here each day on a different problem. When you begin this discipline, you likely will have difficulty identifying problems to work on. After all, we just don't gravitate to problems voluntarily.

During the reading of this book, you have noticed my use of the phrase "problem or situation." This was written deliberately. Many times we don't try to solve something because nothing is apparently wrong. This doesn't mean improvements can't be made, as we know they can. If you can't find a suitable problem to address, then look at a situation that is important to you, and use one of these techniques on it.

Be a "Know It All" In Something

Also contained in an earlier section of this book is the fact that innovative ideas are not produced at random from some unknown stockpile of data. Innovative ideas are actually a merger of ideas from dissimilar fields of our experience. Therefore, a person with more interests tends to be more creative; he or she has a larger knowledge base with which to work.

This cross fertilization of ideas can be encouraged by becoming completely familiar with other disciplines. If you become an expert in the technology of sand casting, it may well benefit your thinking in personal relations. My suggestion for this technique is to choose a field in which you are already interested. You will find it easier to invest the time learning something if you're attracted to the information at the start.

Assume This Is Your First Day on the Job

This little bit of self-trickery has given me more good ideas than any other approach. When you first begin a new job, you see things that you'd like to change. Perhaps they are little things that you're just not comfortable with, or they are actually poor practices which shouldn't be allowed. If you begin tomorrow as though it were the first day on the job, you again look at these practices, but from a more enlightened view. You still know that they are there, but the difference is you also know the proper avenues to take to fix them.

This is one of the best ways I know for parlaying our experience and education rather than hiding behind them. This suggestion was offered earlier in the book, but it deserves to be repeated.

Always Generate at Least Three Alternative Solutions to Any Problem

If the best idea is the result of many, as we have pointed out, then you need to generate many alternative solutions as a matter of habit. The selection of at least three is not offered without cause.

You know you already have one solution to every situation, the "one right answer." According to these instructions, you can't stop at that solution, as it is only one of a group of one. So you offer another alternative. You can't stop at that one either, as it gives us only two alternatives. You have to go to three. While the second alternative wasn't especially hard to come up with (it was probably a lot like the first), the third is more difficult because it may come from another direction.

You could accept the third, but frankly the new direction which option three took you in brought up some other options as well. And so it goes.

Each alternative solution gives you the opportunity to look in other directions for new alternatives. This, in turn, brings to mind other options, etc.

Use "What If..." Once Per Day

This simple technique is not only beneficial, it is a lot of fun as well. Every day look at one situation and ask yourself, "What if..." Then follow that phrase with a statement that is either false or only partially true. Then simply answer the question.

With a little practice, you can invest as little as a few minutes on this, and some interesting conclusions will result.

Practice!

What kind of a self-help book would this be if we didn't point out the need for sacrifice?

In this book we used the analogy of learning long division when describing how to think more creatively. The similarities are apparent when you look at the steps you used to learn this mathematical necessity.

When your teacher first described the procedure for learning long division, you sat there and wondered if there was some way to avoid it entirely. Upon discovering she was sincere about your learning it, you began following her instructions. Through constant repetition you learned how to do it, and passed your test.

The key piece of information in this fascinating trip down memory lane is the idea of constant repetition. Unless you were one of those who could speak Greek at two years old, repetition was absolutely essential to your learning. So it is here as well. I guarantee that none of these tools will work for you under pressure (like your long division test) unless you first master them without pressure (like homework).

You will find that like long division, you soon will be able to apply some of these tools as you stand, just as you can approximate the correct answer to a long division problem without pen and paper. Without the practice, the tools we show you here are nothing more than an interesting sidetrack for you. As important as your creativity is to your personal growth, I hope you have greater regard for it than that.

Chapter Twelve:

Tying It All Together

SUMMARY OF CHAPTER 11:

To assure that our daily routine will now include provisions for innovative thinking, we offered these seven suggestions for your schedule:

A. Change your morning routine, upset your homeostasis!

B. Analyze at least one problem per day.

C. Be a "know-it-all" in something.

D. Assume this is the first day on your job.

E. Always generate at least three alternative solutions to any problem.

F. Use "What if..." once per day.

G. Practice!

OBJECTIVES OF CHAPTER 12:

1. The entire process of innovative thinking revolves around our constant challenges to status quo. This is not instinctive or easy for us. We will present a series of questions that, when answered, will start the challenge process.
2. To better understand how to use the tools in this book in a real-life situation, we will work with you on a problem, using the suggestions presented in this book.

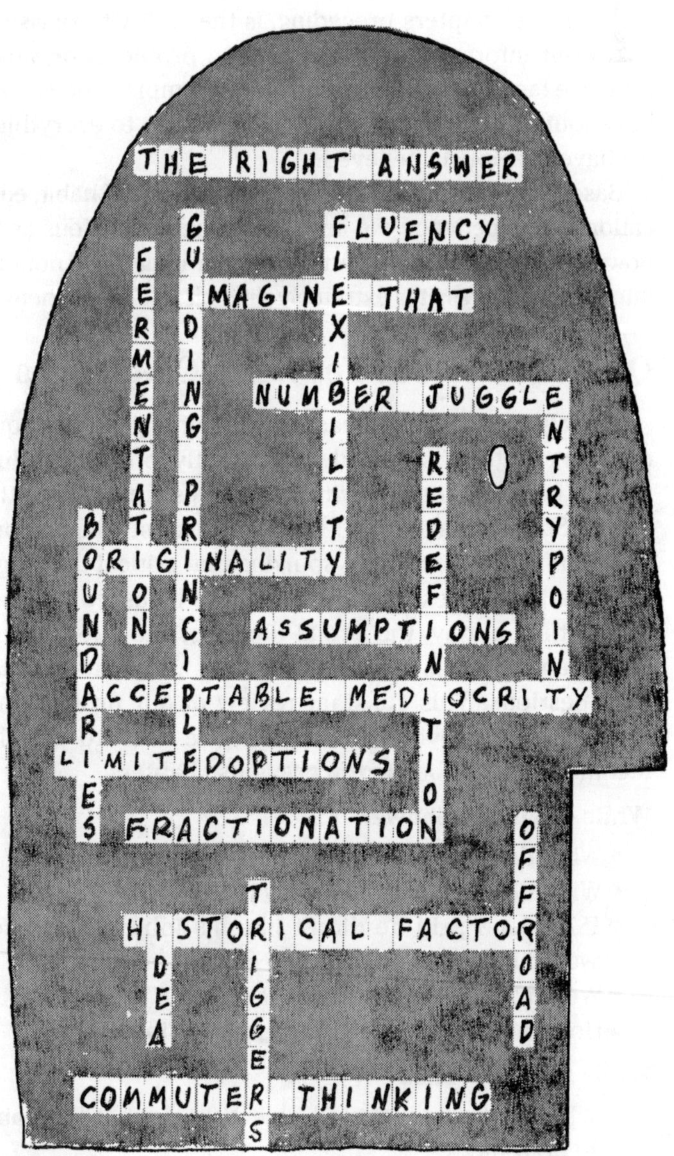
THE RIGHT ANSWER
FLUENCY
IMAGINE THAT
NUMBER JUGGLE
ORIGINALITY
ASSUMPTIONS
ACCEPTABLE MEDIOCRITY
LIMITEDOPTIONS
FRACTIONATION
HISTORICAL FACTOR
COMMUTER THINKING
GUIDING PRINCIPLE
FERMENTATION
FLEXIBILITY
BOUNDARIES
REDEFINITION
ENTRYPOINT
OFFROAD
IDEA
TRIGGERS

The core of creative thinking, as we have indicated in the chapters preceding, is the ability to reassess our information as it applies to problems or situations we face. While this sounds like a simple process, we have found that it is not, for it goes counter to everything we have previously believed.

Based on years, and in some cases decades, of habit, education and experience, we have preconceived notions as to how things are best done. After incorporating these notions into our daily lives, it is extremely difficult to change them.

Questions to Use For Daily Challenges

To help us constantly reassess and intelligently critique our work patterns, we need to constantly look for productive change. In working with executives throughout the United States, I have found the following list of questions to be an invaluable tool for spurring that critical thinking.

While these questions are laid out to be asked at a particular time of day, the actual timing of the query is not significant. What is significant is that we constantly ask the questions. This constant review of our professional patterns will provide the impetus we need to use the techniques described in the previous chapters.

While I'm In the Shower

- What do I love about my job?
- What do I like least about my job?
- If a friend said he didn't like his job, what advice would I give him to help him enjoy it more?
- Would that advice work for me as well?
- How can I help a co-worker enjoy his job more?

While I Eat Breakfast

- What is the one, overall objective of what I'm going to do today?

- If I were given a test on all the tasks I do in my job, which parts would I pass; which parts would I fail?
- Do I enjoy the parts I would pass? The parts I would fail?
- If I were asked to list as many different definitions as I could for my job, what would the list include?

While I Drive to Work

- If I drive to work by a different route today, what can I see that I haven't seen before?
- If I change the order in which I do things, could I do more, do a better job, or do it in less time?

When I Am Doing a Job the Same Way For Years

- What if this job were inside out?
- What has changed in the last five years that impacts on this job? How does, or will, that change the way I do the job?
- How is this job similar to my favorite activity? How is it different?
- If I wrote down a ridiculous way to get this job done, how could I make that new method practical?
- Does this job need to be done at all? How often? The same way every time?

While I'm Relaxing In the Evening

- What is it I want out of my job? How can I begin tomorrow to get that?

While I'm Planning For Tomorrow

- What would happen if I did something backwards tomorrow?
- What boundaries restrict me in doing my job (dollars, time, number of people, schedule, area of facility, etc.)? What can I do about them?
- If I plan tomorrow to have the greatest impact, what would my job consist of? How much of this can I do?

While I'm Doing My Dullest Job

- What small change can I make in this job to make it more palatable?
- What would it take to spur my interest in this job? Can I do that?
- Who said it should be done this way? How long ago? Have things changed since then? What has changed?
- If given the flexibility to do so, how would I change the way this is done?
- If I had two weeks to plan how this job should be done, how would I do it?
- Count how many ways there are to do this job. Why have I chosen to do it this way?

Tying It All Together: A Case Study

While each of the techniques discussed in this book are not difficult to understand, it is sometimes hard to apply new information without a specific example. The case below provides a situation in which we can use these techniques, and our treatment of this case will give you additional understanding of innovation in practice.

Assume that you started your business about eight years ago and, despite the fact that the timing coincided with a relatively serious recession, your growth has been appreciable. From a staff of three family members willing to work long hours for little compensation, you have now grown to a firm of 150 people. There is a good sense of camaraderie among your staff, and a positive outlook as to the company's opportunities in the future.

In the last few months, you have noticed an irritating tendency for mistakes to crop up. In many cases, these mistakes are caused by poor or inadequate information. In one instance, the manufacturing department made a minor change in the product without consulting sales.

The change, it turns out, was important to the sales department, and customers were irritated.

In another instance, the head of human resources had initiated a change in policy based on the best information she had at that time. This change defied one of the promises you had made to your employees years before and, despite the fact that you canceled it immediately, there had been a breach of trust with some of your key employees.

It is your feeling that the growth of your firm is creating the need for rapid and continual change. Unfortunately many of these changes are being made in an informational vacuum. Your people are responsible and professional, but they seem to move without being aware of things that are happening in other departments.

Step One: Write down your definition of this problem

From previous chapters, we know that the definition of the problem is the most logical starting point for finding solutions. Write your definition in the space below.

For our purposes, we chose to define the problem as: poor information flow.

Step Two: List all of the barriers that apply to this problem (i.e., everything you know, or believe to be true, about the problem)

In the space below, list everything you know, or believe to be true, about this problem.

Our list of everything we know, or believe to be true, about this problem is shown below:

- *Our people are competent.*
- *The information is available.*
- *People know where to get the information.*
- *We have the right number of people involved in disseminating and using information.*

- *People want the information.*
- *The problem, as we have defined it, actually exists.*
- *The problem can be solved.*
- *The problem can be solved within the budget.*
- *The problem can be solved with our current staff.*
- *The problem is worth solving.*
- *The information has value.*

Step Three: Challenge every barrier in your list

Recall that if we don't write down our assumptions concerning a situation or problem, they continue to guide our thinking whether or not they are appropriate. Our purpose here is to critically review each barrier to be sure it is appropriate under these circumstances.

Our challenges are shown below.

- *Our people are competent.*

(Probably true, but are they competent to handle a communication problem? Do they have the training or skills necessary? Are they competent to recognize the problem?)

- *The information is available.*

(Also likely true, but do they know where to get it? Do they understand when the information is required to make a good decision?)

- *People know where to get the information.*

(This is likely not true. If they did, they would have requested it.)

- *We have the right number of people involved in disseminating and using the information.*

(Less clear here. Do we have too many people making key decisions? Do we have departments that aren't necessary as independent units?)

- *People want the information.*

(This could be false, many people would prefer to "shoot from the hip.")

- *The problem, as we have defined it, actually exists.*

(We know the consequences exist, but does the problem exist as we have defined it?)

- *The problem can be solved.*

(This is true.)

- *The problem can be solved within the budget.*

(This is also likely true.)

- *The problem can be solved with our current staff.*

(Our natural inclination is to believe this is true, but based on the fact that the problem persists, maybe it is an invalid assumption.)

- *The problem is worth solving.*

(Absolutely true. If we can see the impact of poor communication at our current size, imagine what it will be like after a few more years.)

- *The information has value.*

(The impact of making decisions without the information clearly points out the importance of the information.)

If you have trouble developing a list of statements like the above, try using "Why not?" to help you. In this instance the "Why not?" would be applied to the statement, "We can't solve this." By listing your reasons for believing that the problem cannot be solved, you inadvertently list your preconceived notions about this situation.

Step Four: Use "What if...?"

In the space below, enter at least three false statements, or statements that stretch the truth, about this problem. Then precede each of them with the phrase "What if..."

Now answer the questions you have created.

The "What if..." questions we created are as follows.

What if...we had no department heads?

- *Everyone would have to manage themselves.*
- *Information flow would have to be perfect.*

- *Assigning responsibilities would be very difficult.*
- *We would have a much flatter organization.*
- *The information problem would be much more severe.*
- *Our people would have to be better trained.*

What if...all information came from one source?

- *Everyone in the company would know where to go for necessary data.*
- *That department head would have an inordinate amount of power.*

What if...everyone in the company recognized the problem?

- *The solution could come from the work group.*
- *The employees would have to be brighter than we think they are!*
- *That would mean that we were the last to know!*

Step Five: Change your entry point

We have discussed the idea that we are better at solving our neighbors' problems than our own. Since we are not close to the problem, our perspective gives us insights that our neighbors have a difficult time spotting. By changing our entry point, we give ourselves the advantage of viewing things from a different position.

The easiest way to apply this suggestion is by imagining a perfect conclusion to our problem, and then by listing all of the things that could have caused that perfect conclusion. Below, list every reason you can think of that might have caused this situation.

Things are going smoothly at the company. There have been several situations in the last month where we were able to take advantage of a market opportunity due to immediate information flow. Information-based errors have fallen to zero, and there seems to be an air of mental comfort within the firm.

Reasons for this include:

Step Six: Redefine the problem

Another method we can use to impose a fresh perspective on ourselves is by changing the definition of the problem or situation. If we supply solutions to each of these redefinitions, we will be offering slightly different options for solving our original problem or situation.

List as many different definitions of our problem as you can below.

Our redefinitions include:

- *Too little talking*
- *No information*
- *Information in the wrong place*
- *Too many people needing information*
- *Too many decisions*

Step Seven: Use forced multiples

As we tend to think of only one solution to each of our problems, our ability to force multiple views on ourselves helps develop expanded thinking. The forced multiples tree is one way to impose that characteristic.

Beginning with a statement about the problem, use a separate sheet of paper to develop a forced multiples tree.

Step Eight: Try a number juggle

As we have shown, numbers are the core of rigid thinking. They give the impression of single, completely correct solutions. When we believe that there are single solutions to a problem, we stop looking for better ways to do things. One of the ways we can break our reliance on numbers is to deliberately shift the meaning of those numbers. We do this with the *number juggle*.

Every situation has numbers attached to it, whether or

not those numbers are apparent. The problem we are working on is no different. If we can identify those numbers and deliberately juggle them to create artificial situations, we can force new perspectives.

List all of the numbers that relate to our problem.

Our numbers include these:

- *Number of employees: 150*
- *Number of errors: 2+*
- *Number of years in business: 8*
- *Number of error opportunities: infinite*
- *Number of people making key errors: 2+*

(Note: had our story been more complete, this list could have included numbers for dollar sales, products, unit shipments, customers, channels of distribution, etc.)

Now we mix the numbers to see what the impact might be.

- *What if we had only two employees, but 150 errors. How would that change our approach?*

Step Nine: Force a relationship

The value of forcing a relationship between two totally unrelated items is that it imposes new terms on old situations. The effect can often be a serendipitous benefit. Select an unrelated object, animate or inanimate, and make a list of terms to describe its characteristics. Then for each term, try to relate it to our problem. Do this below.

Since we used an inanimate object in the earlier chapter on this subject, we have chosen to use an animate object in this section. Our object is a wolf, and its characteristics are listed below.

- *Free*
- *Wild*
- *Furry*
- *Family*

- *Approaching extinction*
- *Rarely found in the United States*
- *Grey to brown*
- *Lives in dens*
- *Shy*
- *Reclusive*
- *Fast*
- *Carnivore*
- *Big game hunter*
- *Social*
- *Hierarchical*

In Sum...

Our purpose in the above example was not to dictate the tools you use to spur innovative solutions to this problem, nor to dictate the order in which the tools are to be used. The above is only one approach to solving this, or any, problem.

As you become more comfortable with each of these techniques, my hope is that at least a few of them will become part of your daily work routine. If they do, your opportunity for personal growth will be immeasurably enhanced.

Good luck, and keep in touch!

"Possibilities"

The purpose of this section is to provide some suggestions as to how the exercises at the end of each chapter might be approached. These alternatives are not intended to be any more "right" than any of your ideas. They are only offered as possibilities.

CHAPTER ONE

1. Your "priors" could be:

•Developing new ways to improve our political system.

a. two party system
b. one person, one vote
c. resistance to change
d. self-serving politicians
e. power of public opinion
or...?

•Designing a house.

a. all walls intersect at 90 degree angles
b. wood construction
c. costs related to square footage
d. separation into many rooms
or...?

•The problem of heavy traffic.

a. too many private vehicles
b. too few lanes of road
c. lack of recognition of problem
d. the feeling that the problem is too big to handle
or...?

•A climate of positive reinforcement in your family.

a. attitudes are already set
b. one person is the core of the problem
c. it really isn't necessary
d. we are already positive
or...?

CHAPTER ONE continued

•Reducing bureaucracy where you work.

a. the bureaucracy is too firmly entrenched
b. some people see the bureaucracy as necessary
c. everyone wants the bureaucracy reduced
d. it would take a long time to accomplish
e. bureaucracy is non-productive
or...?

2. Your habits at home could include:

a. eat meals at the same time every day
(Could you take better advantage of the daylight hours with another meal schedule? Would you get more done at work if you took lunch at a different time?)
b. spend little energy making new friends
(Would you profit from knowing more people?)
c. your reaction to questions from your children
(Do you challenge their thought processes, or their right to question you?)
d. the jobs you consider "yours," and those you consider the property of other family members
(Could you learn more by shifting your duties; could your family members learn more also?)
or...?

CHAPTER TWO

1. Things you know, or believe to be true, about dealing with difficult people could include the following:

a. these people have antisocial traits
b. working with them requires patience
c. the patience required may not be worth the effort
d. they are difficult for everyone to deal with, not just you
e. the problem is them, not me
f. they will respond to positive input
or...?

2. Everything you know, or believe to be true, about your problem includes:

a. ______________________________

b. ______________________________

or...?

CHAPTER THREE

1. No response necessary.

2. No response necessary.

3. The "facts" you believe to be true could include the following:

a. the cuts are unattainable
b. more work output equals more people
c. more work output equals more money
d. the cuts in budget include capital expenses
e. the cuts are unwarranted
f. you will run into resistance from your staff
or...?

CHAPTER FOUR

1. Your solutions could include these options:

a. Sit down and emphasize how important follow-up with the customer is. (Commuter Traffic)
b. Fire the sales person. (Off-Road)
c. Change his territory. (Commuter Traffic)
d. Change his job description to match his interests and skills. (Commuter Traffic)
e. Ask him to prepare a seminar on the importance of customer service, to be presented to the other sales people. (Off-Road)

or...?

2. No response necessary.

CHAPTER FIVE

1. Ways to reduce staff expenses could include:

a. encourage mutiny among staff members
b. fire everyone and start all over again
c. merge your department with another department
d. take away all benefits
e. mechanize the entire office function
or...?

2. If I was the most competent person in my field...

a. I'd make a ton of money!
b. I'd be less concerned with survival issues.
c. I'd be at a higher level in my firm.
d. more people would come to me for advice.
e. less of my energy would be spent in self-promotion.
or...?

3. If my employer found a machine to do my work...

a. it would cut down on the attendance at the company picnic.
b. future growth comes from people and ideas, not machines.
c. management tasks would be left to my boss, some of which are basically unattractive.
or...?

CHAPTER SIX

1. Reasons your sale went so well could include:

a. the economy was strong
b. the auto industry was in one of its "up" cycles
c. the weather was beautiful
d. your major competitors went out of business
e. you offer the best vehicles
or...?

2. No response necessary.

CHAPTER SEVEN

1. These definitions will include:

- "Poor sales performance"
  poor performance
  too few customers
  inadequate sales per customer
  too few products
  lack of sales skill
  or...?
- "Out-of-control budget"
  poor budget
  expenses exceeding budget
  out-of-control expenses
  loss of control in budget area
  or...?
- "Our people don't see how they will benefit"
  our people don't see
  our people won't benefit
  lack of understanding
  clear understanding of a lack of benefit
  or...?

2. An example of expanded definition could be:

"Poor sales performance"

The sales of products 1, 2, 3, and 4 are off 23% from this same time period last year. This decline has been concentrated in the central region of the country, and was first evident during September of this year. The decline was initially precipitous, but stabilized at more than 20% after the first few months. The decline has not worsened in the last two months.

or...?

3. No response necessary.

CHAPTER EIGHT

1. No response necessary.

2. No response necessary.

CHAPTER NINE

1. Poor morale among employees

a. number of employees
b. number of morale complaints
c. days absent
d. measures of quality of work
e. turnover
or...?

An attitude problem in a department

a. number of employee complaints
b. number of employees
c. number of changes in the department
or...?

A lack of "vision" on the part of your employees

a. number of employees
b. number of employees affected
c. required number of "visions" per employee
or...?

2. No response necessary.

CHAPTER TEN

1. No response necessary.

2. No response necessary.

Index